PRAISE FOR
MODELING AND SIMULA

"Downey uses a combination of Python, calculus, besp
and easily accessible online materials to model a diverse and m.
of simulation projects. In the process, he presents a practical and reusable
framework for modeling dynamical systems with Python."

—LEE VAUGHAN, AUTHOR OF *PYTHON TOOLS
FOR SCIENTISTS*, *REAL-WORLD PYTHON*,
AND *IMPRACTICAL PYTHON PROJECTS* AND
FORMER SENIOR PRINCIPAL SCIENTIST AT
EXXONMOBIL

"*Modeling and Simulation in Python* is an introduction to physical modeling
using a computational approach [which] makes it possible to work with
more realistic models than what you typically see in a first-year physics class."

—PYTHON KITCHEN

"An impressive introduction to physical modeling and Python programming,
featuring clear, concise explanations and examples . . . perfect for readers of
any level."

—CHRISTIAN MAYER, AUTHOR OF *PYTHON
ONE-LINERS* AND FOUNDER OF FINXTER.COM

"*Modeling and Simulation in Python* provides a wealth of instructive examples
of all kinds of modeling. . . . This book can be valuable as a textbook for
classes on scientific computation or as a guide to exploration for interested
amateurs."

—BRADFORD TUCKFIELD, AUTHOR OF *DIVE
INTO ALGORITHMS* AND *DIVE INTO DATA SCIENCE*

"Downey's book fills a significant gap in the market. For those unwilling to
commit to the prolonged dullness of a bottom-up approach to programming,
Downey's top-down, context-rich, and motivating approach dramatically
lowers the barrier to gaining literacy in programming and explicitly and
insightfully teaches modeling."

—PHAT VU, DIRECTOR OF THE SCIENCE
AND MATHEMATICS PROGRAM AT SOKA
UNIVERSITY OF AMERICA

MODELING AND SIMULATION IN PYTHON

An Introduction for Scientists and Engineers

by Allen B. Downey

no starch
press

San Francisco

Printed in the United States of America

27 26 25 24 23   1 2 3 4 5

ISBN-13: 978-1-7185-0216-1 (print)
ISBN-13: 978-1-7185-0217-8 (ebook)

Publisher: William Pollock
Managing Editor: Jill Franklin
Production Manager: Sabrina Plomitallo-González
Production Editor: Jennifer Kepler
Developmental Editor: Alex Freed
Cover Illustrator: Gina Redman
Interior Design: Octopod Studios
Technical Reviewer: Valerie Barr
Copyeditor: Gary Smith
Proofreader: Lisa Devoto Farrell

For information on distribution, bulk sales, corporate sales, or translations, please contact No Starch Press, Inc. directly at info@nostarch.com or:

No Starch Press, Inc.
245 8th Street, San Francisco, CA 94103
phone: 1.415.863.9900
www.nostarch.com

Library of Congress Control Number: 2022049830

[S]

About the Author

Allen Downey is a staff scientist at DrivenData and professor emeritus at Olin College, where he taught Modeling and Simulation and other classes related to software and data science. He is the author of several textbooks, including *Think Python*, *Think Bayes*, and *Elements of Data Science*. Previously, he taught at Wellesley College and Colby College. He received his PhD in computer science from the University of California, Berkeley, in 1997. His undergraduate and master's degrees are from the civil engineering department at MIT. He is the author of *Probably Overthinking It*, a blog about data science and Bayesian statistics.

About the Technical Reviewer

Valerie Barr has spent more than a decade focusing on interdisciplinary applications and curricular strategies to expose students from all fields to computing. This has included developing and offering courses in modeling and simulation, data visualization, and other areas that now also cross into data science. She has a PhD in computer science from Rutgers University, held the Jean Sammet Chair at Mount Holyoke College, and now holds the Margaret Hamilton Chair at Bard College, where she is launching the Bard Network Computing Initiative.

BRIEF CONTENTS

Acknowledgments xvii
Introduction xix

PART I: DISCRETE SYSTEMS

Chapter 1: Introduction to Modeling 3
Chapter 2: Modeling a Bike Share System 15
Chapter 3: Iterative Modeling 27
Chapter 4: Parameters and Metrics 35
Chapter 5: Building a Population Model 43
Chapter 6: Iterating the Population Model 53
Chapter 7: Limits to Growth 61
Chapter 8: Projecting into the Future 69
Chapter 9: Analysis and Symbolic Computation 79
Chapter 10: Case Studies Part I 89

PART II: FIRST-ORDER SYSTEMS

Chapter 11: Epidemiology and SIR Models 95
Chapter 12: Quantifying Interventions 105
Chapter 13: Sweeping Parameters 111
Chapter 14: Nondimensionalization 119
Chapter 15: Thermal Systems 127
Chapter 16: Solving the Coffee Problem 137
Chapter 17: Modeling Blood Sugar 145
Chapter 18: Implementing the Minimal Model 153
Chapter 19: Case Studies Part II 163

PART III: SECOND-ORDER SYSTEMS

Chapter 20: The Falling Penny Revisited 171
Chapter 21: Drag 177
Chapter 22: Two-Dimensional Motion 185

Chapter 23: Optimization 199
Chapter 24: Rotation 205
Chapter 25: Torque. 215
Chapter 26: Case Studies Part III 227

Appendix: Under the Hood. 235

Index. 243

CONTENTS IN DETAIL

ACKNOWLEDGMENTS   xvii

INTRODUCTION   xix

Who Is This Book For? xx
     How Much Math and Science Do I Need? xx
     How Much Programming Do I Need? xxi
Book Overview... xxi
Teaching Modeling xxiv
Getting Started xxv
     Installing Python xxv
     Running Jupyter xxvi
Suggestions and Corrections... xxvi

PART I
DISCRETE SYSTEMS

1
INTRODUCTION TO MODELING   3

The Modeling Framework 3
Testing the Falling Penny Myth 5
Computation in Python 6
     False Precision 7
     Computation with Units 8
Summary 10
Exercises 11

2
MODELING A BIKE SHARE SYSTEM   15

Our Bike Share Model 15
Defining Functions 17
Print Statements 18
if Statements 19
Parameters 21
for Loops 22
TimeSeries 22
Plotting 24

Summary 24
Exercises 25
Under the Hood 25

3
ITERATIVE MODELING   27

Iterating on Our Bike Share Model 27
Using More Than One State Object 28
Documentation 29
Dealing with Negative Bikes 30
Comparison Operators 31
Introducing Metrics 32
Summary 33
Exercises 33

4
PARAMETERS AND METRICS   35

Functions That Return Values 35
Loops and Arrays 37
Sweeping Parameters 38
Incremental Development 40
Summary 40
Exercises 41
Challenge Exercises 41
Under the Hood 42

5
BUILDING A POPULATION MODEL   43

Exploring the Data 44
Absolute and Relative Errors 47
Modeling Population Growth 48
Simulating Population Growth 50
Summary 51
Exercise 52

6
ITERATING THE POPULATION MODEL   53

System Objects 53
A Proportional Growth Model 56
Factoring Out the Update Function 57

Combining Birth and Death.. 58
Summary 59
Exercise 59
Under the Hood 59

7
LIMITS TO GROWTH   **61**

Quadratic Growth.. 62
Net Growth.. 63
Finding Equilibrium 65
Dysfunctions 65
Summary 68
Exercises 68

8
PROJECTING INTO THE FUTURE   **69**

Generating Projections 69
Comparing Projections 72
Summary 74
Exercise 74

9
ANALYSIS AND SYMBOLIC COMPUTATION   **79**

Difference Equations 79
Differential Equations 80
Analysis and Simulation 82
Analysis with WolframAlpha 83
Analysis with SymPy 83
Differential Equations in SymPy 84
Solving the Quadratic Growth Model.. 86
Summary 87
Exercises 88

10
CASE STUDIES PART I   **89**

Historical World Population 89
One Queue or Two?... 90
Predicting Salmon Populations 91
Tree Growth 91

PART II
FIRST-ORDER SYSTEMS

11
EPIDEMIOLOGY AND SIR MODELS 95

The Freshman Plague 95
The Kermack-McKendrick Model 96
The KM Equations 97
Implementing the KM Model 98
The Update Function 99
Running the Simulation 100
Collecting the Results 101
Now with a TimeFrame 103
Summary 104
Exercise 104

12
QUANTIFYING INTERVENTIONS 105

The Effects of Immunization 105
Choosing Metrics 107
Sweeping Immunization 108
Summary 110
Exercise 110

13
SWEEPING PARAMETERS 111

Sweeping Beta 111
Sweeping Gamma 113
Using a SweepFrame 114
Summary 117
Exercise 118

14
NONDIMENSIONALIZATION 119

Beta and Gamma 119
Exploring the Results 120
Contact Number 122
Comparing Analysis and Simulation 123
Estimating the Contact Number 124
Summary 125
Exercises 125
Under the Hood 126

15
THERMAL SYSTEMS

127

The Coffee Cooling Problem 127
Temperature and Heat 128
Heat Transfer 129
Newton's Law of Cooling 129
Implementing Newtonian Cooling 130
Finding Roots 134
Estimating r 135
Summary 136
Exercises 136

16
SOLVING THE COFFEE PROBLEM

137

Mixing Liquids 138
Mix First or Last? 139
Optimal Timing 140
The Analytic Solution 141
Summary 143
Exercises 143

17
MODELING BLOOD SUGAR

145

The Minimal Model 146
The Glucose Minimal Model 146
Getting the Data 148
Interpolation 149
Summary 150
Exercises 151

18
IMPLEMENTING THE MINIMAL MODEL

153

Implementing the Model 154
The Update Function 154
Running the Simulation 156
Solving Differential Equations 158
Summary 162
Exercise 162

19
CASE STUDIES PART II

163

Revisiting the Minimal Model 163
The Insulin Minimal Model 164

Low-Pass Filter 164
Thermal Behavior of a Wall 166
HIV 167

PART III
SECOND-ORDER SYSTEMS

20
THE FALLING PENNY REVISITED 171

Newton's Second Law of Motion 171
Dropping Pennies 172
Event Functions 175
Summary 176
Exercise 176

21
DRAG 177

Calculating Drag Force 177
The Params Object 179
Simulating the Penny Drop 180
Summary 183
Exercises 183

22
TWO-DIMENSIONAL MOTION 185

Assumptions and Decisions 185
Vectors 186
Simulating Baseball Flight 189
Drag Force 191
Adding an Event Function 192
Visualizing Trajectories 194
Animating the Baseball 196
Summary 196
Exercises 196

23
OPTIMIZATION 199

The Manny Ramirez Problem 200
Finding the Range 201
Summary 203
Exercise 204
Under the Hood 204

24
ROTATION   205

The Physics of Toilet Paper 206
Setting Parameters.. 207
Simulating the System 208
Plotting the Results 210
The Analytic Solution 212
Summary 213
Exercise 214

25
TORQUE   215

Angular Acceleration 215
Moment of Inertia 216
Teapots and Turntables 216
Two-Phase Simulation 219
        Phase 1 220
        Phase 2 220
        Combining the Results 221
Estimating Friction 223
Animating the Turntable 225
Summary 226
Exercise 226

26
CASE STUDIES PART III   227

Bungee Jumping... 227
Bungee Dunk Revisited 228
Orbiting the Sun 229
Spider-Man 229
Kittens... 230
Simulating a Yo-Yo 231
Congratulations 233

APPENDIX: UNDER THE HOOD   235

How run_solve_ivp Works... 236
How root_scalar Works 239
How maximize_scalar Works... 240

INDEX   243

ACKNOWLEDGMENTS

My early work on this book benefited from conversations with my colleagues at Olin College, including John Geddes, Mark Somerville, Alison Wood, Chris Lee, and Jason Woodard.

I am grateful to Lisa Downey and Jason Woodard for their thoughtful and careful copyediting, and to Eoghan Downey and Jason Moore for their technical review.

Thanks to Alessandra Ferzoco, Erhardt Graeff, Emily Tow, Kelsey Houston-Edwards, Linda Vanasupa, Matt Neal, Joanne Pratt, and Steve Matsumoto for their helpful suggestions.

INTRODUCTION

 This book is about *dynamical systems*, that is, things that change over time. The first example we'll look at is a penny falling from the Empire State Building, where the thing that's changing is the position of the penny in space. Other examples include a cup of coffee, where temperature changes over time, and glucose in the human bloodstream, where concentration changes over time.

We will define models, which are simplifications intended to include the most important elements of the real world and leave out the least important, and we will write Python programs that simulate these models. We will use models and simulations to do three kinds of work: predicting how a system will behave, explaining why it behaves as it does, and designing systems to behave the way we want.

If you have taken an introductory physics class, you have seen models of dynamical systems. For example, you might have modeled a block on a plane, a projectile, or a planet in orbit.

If you took a good class, you were aware of the decisions those models were based on. Most likely the model of the block did not include friction, the model of the projectile did not include air resistance, and the model of the planet was a "point mass."

And if you took a very good class, you were also aware of the limitations of these models. For example, in many real-world systems, friction and air resistance are among the most important elements; if you leave them out of the model, your predictions will not be accurate and your designs will not work. On the other hand, a model that treats a planet as a point mass is good enough to compute orbits with high accuracy.

But most physics classes are based on mathematical analysis, which makes it hard to work with elements like friction and air resistance. That's why the focus of this book is computational simulation, which makes it possible to work with more realistic models and to try out different models. With a computational approach, we can also take on a wide variety of systems. Examples in this book include a bike share system, world population growth, and queueing systems; epidemics, electronic circuits, and external walls; baseballs and bungee jumpers; and turntables and yo-yos.

I hope you will find this approach interesting, empowering, and at least a little bit fun.

Who Is This Book For?

If you are studying or working in the natural or social sciences, this book will help you think about models and the work we can do with them. I hope there's at least one model in this book that is related to your field, but even if not, the lessons you learn about modeling apply to almost every field.

How Much Math and Science Do I Need?

I'll assume that you know what derivatives and integrals are, but that's about all. In particular, you don't need to know (or remember) much about finding derivatives or integrals of functions analytically. If you know the derivative of x^2 and you can integrate $2x\,dx$, that will do it. More importantly, you should understand what those concepts *mean*; but if you don't, this book might help you figure it out. You don't have to know anything about differential equations.

As for science, we will cover topics from a variety of fields, including demography, epidemiology, medicine, thermodynamics, and mechanics. For the most part, I don't assume you know anything about these topics. But one of the skills you will develop is the ability to learn enough about new fields to develop models and simulations.

When we get to mechanics, I'll assume you understand the relationship between position, velocity, and acceleration, and that you are familiar with Newton's laws of motion, especially the second law, which is often expressed as $F = ma$ (force equals mass times acceleration).

How Much Programming Do I Need?

If you have never programmed before, you should be able to read this book, understand it, and do the exercises. I will do my best to explain everything you need to know; in particular, I have carefully chosen the vocabulary I introduce, and I try to define each term the first time it is used.

In this book, you learn to program with an immediate goal in mind: writing simulations of physical systems. And we proceed "top down," by which I mean we use professional-strength data structures and language features right away. In particular, we use the following Python libraries:

- NumPy for numerical computation (*https://www.numpy.org*)
- SciPy for scientific computation (*https://www.scipy.org*)
- Matplotlib for visualization (*https://matplotlib.org*)
- pandas for working with data (*https://pandas.pydata.org*)
- SymPy for symbolic computation (*https://www.sympy.org*)
- Pint for units like kilograms and meters (*https://pint.readthedocs.io*)
- Jupyter for reading, running, and developing code (*https://jupyter.org*)

These tools let you work on more interesting programs sooner, but there are some drawbacks: they can be hard to use, and it can be challenging to keep track of which library does what and how they interact. I have tried to mitigate these problems by providing a ModSim library that makes it easier to get started with these tools and provides some additional capabilities.

Some features in the ModSim library are like training wheels; at some point you will probably stop using them and start working with the underlying libraries directly. Other features you might find useful the whole time you are working through the book, and later. I encourage you to read the ModSim library code. Most of it is not complicated, and I tried to make it readable. Particularly if you have some programming experience, you might learn something by reverse engineering my design decisions.

Book Overview

This book is organized into three parts. Part I is about systems made up of discrete components; examples include a bike sharing system and population growth. The chapters in this part are as follows:

Chapter 1: Introduction to Modeling   This chapter introduces the modeling framework and demonstrates it by testing the falling penny myth. It also presents Pint, a library for computation with units like meters and kilograms.

Chapter 2: Modeling a Bike Share System   This chapter applies the modeling framework to a bike share system and introduces some of the programming tools we'll need throughout the book, including functions, loops, and the TimeSeries data structure.

Chapter 3: Iterative Modeling   This chapter demonstrates the iterative modeling process by gradually improving our model of the bike share system. It uses State objects to track the bicycles and checks for impossible conditions like negative bikes.

Chapter 4: Parameters and Metrics   We put the bike share model to work, using it to predict the behavior of the system under a range of conditions, like changes in customer demand. We also suggest ways to test and debug code.

Chapter 5: Building a Population Model   This is the first of five chapters about world population growth. It starts with data from the last 50 years and tests several models to see if they fit the data.

Chapter 6: Iterating the Population Model   Here we incrementally improve our population model, making it more realistic and making the code easier to read and modify. We also introduce System objects that represent information about the system we're modeling.

Chapter 7: Limits to Growth   In this chapter we add new features to the model to represent the limits of population growth and suggest ways to test and debug functions.

Chapter 8: Projecting into the Future   Here we continue our work on world population by generating projections for the next 80 years and comparing them to projections from professional demographers.

Chapter 9: Analysis and Symbolic Computation   This chapter presents mathematical methods for analyzing our world population models and introduces SymPy, a library for doing symbolic computation. This chapter should interest people who like mathematical analysis, but it's optional: if you choose to skip it, you won't miss out on anything you need later in the book.

Chapter 10: Case Studies Part I   This chapter presents four case studies that apply the methods we've learned so far to a diverse set of topics: prehistoric world population, wildlife population, tree growth, and queueing systems.

Part II is about systems that can be described by first-order differential equations, including objects that heat up and cool down, chemical concentrations and reactions, and the transmission of infectious disease. Here's a breakdown of the chapters:

Chapter 11: Epidemiology and SIR Models   The first of four chapters on modeling infectious disease, it introduces the SIR model and the TimeFrame data structure.

Chapter 12: Quantifying Interventions   This chapter uses the SIR model to quantify the effect of interventions like quarantine and immunization on infectious disease and explores the phenomenon of herd immunity.

Chapter 13: Sweeping Parameters   This chapter explores the effect of infection and recovery rates on the progress of an infectious disease and introduces the `SweepFrame` data structure.

Chapter 14: Nondimensionalization   Here we conclude our work with the SIR model. We use mathematical analysis to understand the relationship between infection rate, recovery rate, and the basic reproduction number, which quantifies the contagiousness of a disease. This chapter is optional.

Chapter 15: Thermal Systems   The first of two chapters about thermal systems, it introduces the coffee cooling problem, which explores the relationship between temperature and heat flow.

Chapter 16: Solving the Coffee Problem   We complete the coffee cooling problem by modeling the mixture of coffee and milk at different temperatures to find the optimal time to mix.

Chapter 17: Modeling Blood Sugar   This is the first of two chapters that explore the regulation of blood sugar by modeling the interaction of glucose and insulin in the human body. It introduces the concept of interpolation.

Chapter 18: Implementing the Minimal Model   We implement the glucose-insulin model using an ODE solver, a numerical method for working with differential equations.

Chapter 19: Case Studies Part II   This chapter presents case studies that apply the tools we've learned so far to a variety of problems, including an electrical circuit, a thermally insulating wall, and the interaction of HIV and the immune system.

Part III is about systems described by second-order differential equations, including objects that move and rotate in space. Examples include projectiles like a baseball and rotating objects like a yo-yo. The chapters are as follows:

Chapter 20: The Falling Penny Revisited   We return to the falling penny example from Chapter 1, this time using an ODE solver to model a projectile moving in one dimension.

Chapter 21: Drag   We extend the falling penny model to include drag due to air resistance; without it, the results are not even close to accurate.

Chapter 22: Two-Dimensional Motion   We move from one dimension to two in order to model the flight of a baseball, including the effect of air resistance. We visualize the results using simple animations.

Chapter 23: Optimization   We conclude the baseball example by solving an optimization question: What is the minimum effort required to hit a home run in Fenway Park?

Chapter 24: Rotation The first of two chapters on rotation, it presents the concept of angular velocity and applies it to the example of manufacturing a roll of toilet paper.

Chapter 25: Torque This chapter introduces the concepts of torque and angular acceleration, making it possible to model systems that involve force and rotation.

Chapter 26: Case Studies Part III This chapter presents six case studies that apply what we've learned to a variety of systems, including a bungee jumper, a yo-yo, Spider-Man, and a kitten unrolling toilet paper.

At the end of each chapter, we provide at least one exercise where you can apply what you have learned. At the end of each part, we present case studies where you can work on a wider variety of problems.

Finally, the appendix "opens the hood" and explains the details of some of the methods we've used, including the ODE solver, the root finder, and the optimizer.

Teaching Modeling

The essential skills of modeling—abstraction, analysis, simulation, and validation—are central in engineering, natural sciences, social sciences, medicine, and many other fields. Some students learn these skills implicitly, but in most schools they are not taught explicitly, and students get little practice. That's the problem this book is meant to address.

At Olin College, we teach these skills in a class called Modeling and Simulation, which all students take in their first semester. I developed this class with my colleagues John Geddes and Mark Somerville and taught it for the first time in 2009. It is based on our belief that modeling should be taught explicitly, early, and throughout the curriculum. It is also based on our conviction that computation is an essential part of this process. If students are limited to the mathematical analysis they can do by hand, they are restricted to a small number of simple physical systems, like a projectile moving in a vacuum or a block on a frictionless plane. And they see a lot of bad models—that is, models that are too simple for their intended purpose.

In most introductory physics classes, students don't make modeling decisions; sometimes they are not even aware of the decisions that have been made for them. Our goal is to teach the entire modeling process and give students a chance to practice it.

Also, we think it is valuable to teach programming and modeling at the same time, rather than require programming as a prerequisite. Most programming classes go "bottom up," starting with basic language features and gradually adding more powerful tools. As a result, it's a long time before students can do anything more interesting than convert Fahrenheit to Celsius. And often they have no context. Students learn to program with no particular goal in mind, so the examples span an incoherent collection of topics, and the exercises tend to be unmotivated. If students learn about programming and modeling early, they can apply those skills throughout the curriculum.

Getting Started

To run the examples and work on the exercises in this book, you will need an environment where you can run Jupyter notebooks. Jupyter is a software development environment where you can write and run Python code. A Jupyter notebook is a document that contains text, code, and results from running the code. Each chapter of this book is a Jupyter notebook where you can run the examples and work on exercises.

To run the notebooks, you have two options:

1. You can install Python and Jupyter on your computer and download the notebooks.

2. You can run the notebooks on Colab, which is a free online service provided by Google.

To run the notebooks on Colab, go to the landing page for this book at *https://allendowney.github.io/ModSimPy* and follow the links to the chapters.

To run the notebooks on your computer, there are three steps:

1. Download the notebooks and copy them to your computer.

2. Install Python, Jupyter, and some additional libraries.

3. Run Jupyter and open the notebooks.

To get the notebooks, download the ZIP archive from *http://modsimpy .com/zip*. You will need a program like WinZip or gzip to unpack the ZIP file. Make a note of the location of the files you unpack.

The next two sections provide details for the other steps. Installing and running software can be challenging, especially if you are not familiar with the command line. If you run into problems, you might want to work on Colab, at least to get started.

Installing Python

To install Python, I recommend you use Anaconda, which is a free Python distribution that includes all the libraries you need for this book (and more). Anaconda is available for Linux, macOS, and Windows. By default, it puts all files in your home directory, so you don't need administrator (root) permission to install it, and if you have a version of Python already, Anaconda will not remove or modify it.

Start at *https://www.anaconda.com/download*. Download the installer for your system and run it. I recommend you run the installer as a normal user, not as administrator or root. I suggest you accept the recommended options. On Windows you have the option to install Visual Studio Code, which is an interactive environment for writing programs. You won't need it for this book, but you might want it for other projects.

By default, Anaconda installs most of the packages you need, but there are a few more you have to add. Once the installation is complete, open a command window. On macOS or Linux, you can use Terminal. On Windows, open the Anaconda Prompt that should be in your Start menu.

Run the following command (copy and paste it if you can, to avoid typos):

```
$ conda install jupyter pandas sympy beautifulsoup4 lxml html5lib
$ conda install -c unidata pint
```

That should install everything you need.

Running Jupyter

If you haven't used Jupyter before, you can read about it at *https://jupyter.org*. To start Jupyter on macOS or Linux, open a Terminal window; on Windows, open the Anaconda Prompt. Use cd to "change directory" into the directory that contains the notebooks:

```
$ cd ModSimPy
```

Then launch the Jupyter notebook server:

```
$ jupyter notebook
```

Jupyter should open a window in a browser, and you should see the list of the notebooks you downloaded. Click on the first notebook, and follow the instructions to run the code. The first time you run a notebook, it might take several seconds to start while some Python files are initialized. After that, it should run faster.

You can also launch Jupyter from the Start menu on Windows, the Dock on macOS, or the Anaconda Navigator on any system. If you do that, Jupyter might start in your home directory or somewhere else in your file system, so you might have to navigate to find the directory with the notebooks.

Suggestions and Corrections

If you have a suggestion or correction, send it to *downey@allendowney.com*. Or if you are a Git user, open an issue or send me a pull request on *https://github.com/AllenDowney/ModSimPy*.

If you include at least part of the sentence the error appears in, that makes it easy for me to search. Page numbers are fine, too, but not as easy to work with. Thanks!

PART I

DISCRETE SYSTEMS

1

INTRODUCTION TO MODELING

 This chapter introduces the modeling framework we will use throughout the book and works through our first example, using a simple model of physics to evaluate the claim that a penny falling from the height of the Empire State Building could kill someone if it hit them on the head. You'll also see how to do computation in Python with units like meters and seconds.

This chapter is available as a Jupyter notebook where you can read the text, run the code, and work on the exercises. You can access the notebooks at *https://allendowney.github.io/ModSimPy*.

The Modeling Framework

This book is about modeling and simulating physical systems. Figure 1-1 shows what I mean by *modeling*.

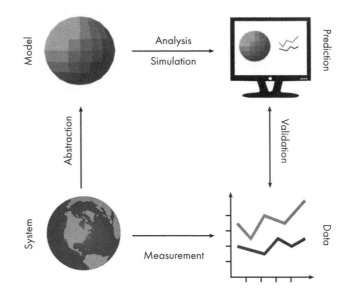

Figure 1-1: The modeling framework for physical systems

Starting in the lower left, the *system* is something in the real world we are interested in. To model the system, we have to decide which elements of the real world to include and which we can leave out. This process is called *abstraction*.

The result of abstraction is a *model*, which is a description of the system that includes only the features we think are essential. A model can be represented in the form of diagrams and equations, which can be used for mathematical *analysis*. It can also be implemented in the form of a computer program, which can run *simulations*.

The result of analysis and simulation might be a *prediction* about what the system will do, an *explanation* of why it behaves the way it does, or a *design* intended to achieve a purpose.

We can *validate* predictions and test designs by taking *measurements* from the real world and comparing the *data* we get with the results from analysis and simulation.

For any physical system, there are many possible models, each one including and excluding different features, or including different levels of detail. The goal of the modeling process is to find the model best suited to its purpose (prediction, explanation, or design). Sometimes the best model is the most detailed. If we include more features, the model is more realistic, and we expect its predictions to be more accurate. But often a simpler model is better. If we include only the essential features and leave out the rest, we get models that are easier to work with, and the explanations they provide can be clearer and more compelling.

As an example, suppose someone asks you why the orbit of the Earth is elliptical. If you model the Earth and Sun as point masses (ignoring their actual size), compute the gravitational force between them using Newton's law of universal gravitation, and compute the resulting orbit using Newton's laws of motion, you can show that the result is an ellipse. Of course, the actual orbit of Earth is not a perfect ellipse, because of the gravitational forces of the Moon, Jupiter, and other objects in the solar system, and because Newton's laws of motion are only approximately true (they don't take into account relativistic effects). But adding these features to the model would not improve the explanation; more detail would only be a distraction from the fundamental cause. However, if the goal is to predict the position of the Earth with great precision, including more details might be necessary.

Choosing the best model depends on what the model is for. It is usually a good idea to start with a simple model, even if it is likely to be too simple, and test whether it is good enough for its purpose. Then you can add features gradually, starting with the ones you expect to be most essential. This process is called *iterative modeling*.

Comparing the results of successive models provides a form of *internal validation*, so you can catch conceptual, mathematical, and software errors. And by adding and removing features, you can tell which ones have the biggest effect on the results and which can be ignored. Comparing results to data from the real world provides *external validation*, which is generally the strongest test.

The modeling framework is pretty abstract; the following example might make it clearer.

Testing the Falling Penny Myth

You might have heard that a penny dropped from the top of the Empire State Building would be going so fast when it hit the pavement that it would be embedded in the concrete; or if it hit a person, it would break their skull.

We can test this myth by making and analyzing two models. For the first model, we'll assume that the effect of air resistance is small. In that case, the primary force acting on the penny is gravity, which causes the penny to accelerate downward.

If the initial velocity is 0 and the acceleration, a, is constant, the velocity after t seconds is:

$$v = at$$

and the distance the penny has dropped is:

$$x = at^2/2$$

To find the time until the penny reaches the sidewalk, we can solve for t:

$$t = \sqrt{2x/a}$$

Plugging in the acceleration of gravity, $a = 9.8 \text{ m/s}^2$, and the height of the Empire State Building, $x = 381$ m, we get $t = 8.8$ s. Then, computing $v = at$, we get a velocity on impact of 86 m/s, which is about 190 miles per hour. That sounds like it could hurt.

Of course, these results are not exact because the model is based on simplifications. For example, we assume that gravity is constant. In fact, the force of gravity is different on different parts of the globe, and it gets weaker as you move away from the surface. But these differences are small, so ignoring them is probably a good choice for this problem.

On the other hand, ignoring air resistance is not a good choice, because in this scenario its effect is substantial. Once the penny gets to about 29 m/s, the upward force of air resistance equals the downward force of gravity, so the penny stops accelerating. This is the *terminal velocity* of the penny in air.

And that suggests a second model, where the penny accelerates until it reaches terminal velocity; after that, acceleration is 0 and velocity is constant. In this model, the penny hits the sidewalk at about 29 m/s. That's much less than 86 m/s, which is what the first model predicts. Getting hit with a penny at that speed might hurt, but it would be unlikely to cause real harm. And it would not damage concrete.

The statistician George Box famously said, "All models are wrong, but some are useful." He was talking about statistical models, but his wise words apply to all kinds of models. Our first model, which ignores air resistance, is very wrong and probably not useful. The second model, which takes air resistance into account, is still wrong, but it's better, and it's good enough to refute the myth.

NOTE *The television show* MythBusters *has tested the myth of the falling penny more carefully; you can view the results at* https://www.youtube.com/watch?v=sJkdNnHhaoI. *Their work is based on a mathematical model of motion, measurements to determine the force of air resistance on a penny, and a physical model of a human head.*

Computation in Python

Let's compute the results from the previous section using Python. First we'll create a variable to represent acceleration due to gravity in meters per second squared (m/s^2):

```
a = 9.8
```

A *variable* is a name that corresponds to a value. In this example, the name is a and the value is the number 9.8.

Suppose we let the penny drop for 3.4 seconds (s). Let's create a variable to represent this time:

```
t = 3.4
```

Now we can compute the velocity of the penny after t seconds:

```
v = a * t
```

Python uses the symbol * for multiplication. The other arithmetic operators include the following symbols: + for addition, - for subtraction, / for division, and ** for exponentiation.

After you assign a value to a variable, you can display the value like this (in examples like this, the code is above the dotted line and the output below):

```
v
```

```
33.32
```

After 3.4 s, the velocity of the penny is about 33 m/s (ignoring air resistance).

Now let's see how far it would travel during that time:

```
x = a * t**2 / 2
x
```

```
56.644
```

It would travel about 56 m.

Now, going in the other direction, let's compute the time it takes to fall 381 m, the height of the Empire State Building:

```
h = 381
```

For this computation, we need the square root function, sqrt, which is provided by a library called NumPy. Before we can use it, we have to import it like this:

```
from numpy import sqrt
```

Now we can use it like this:

```
t = sqrt(2 * h / a)
t
```

```
8.817885349720552
```

With no air resistance, it would take about 8.8 s for the penny to reach the sidewalk.

Finally, let's calculate its velocity:

```
v = a * t
v
```

```
86.41527642726142
```

The velocity on impact would be about 86 m/s.

False Precision

Python displays results with about 16 digits, which gives the impression that they are very precise, but don't be fooled. The numbers we get out are only as good as the numbers we put in.

For example, the "roof height" of the Empire State Building is 380 m. I chose $h = 381$ m for this example on the assumption that the observation deck is on the roof and you drop the penny from a 1 m railing. But that's probably not right, so we should treat this value as an approximation where only the first two digits are likely to be right.

If the precision of the inputs is two digits, the precision of the outputs is two digits, *at most*. That's why, if the output is `86.41527642726142`, I report it as "about 86."

Computation with Units

The computations we just did use numbers without units. When we set `h = 381`, we left out the meters, and when we set `a = 9.8`, we left out the meters per second squared. And, when we got the result `v = 86`, we added back the meters per second.

Leaving units out of computation is a common practice, but it tends to cause errors, including the very expensive failure of the Mars Climate Orbiter in 1999 (*https://en.wikipedia.org/wiki/Mars_Climate_Orbiter*). When possible, it is better to include units in the computation.

To represent units, we'll use a library called Pint, which you can read about at *https://pint.readthedocs.io*. To use it, we have to import a function called `UnitRegistry` and call it like this:

```
from pint import UnitRegistry

units = UnitRegistry()
```

The result is an object that contains variables representing pretty much every unit you've heard of. For example:

```
units.league
```
```
league
```

or:

```
units.fortnight
```
```
fortnight
```

But leagues and fortnights are not part of the International System of Units; in the jargon, they are not *SI units*. Instead, we will use `meter`

```
meter = units.meter
meter
```
```
meter
```

and second:

```
second = units.second
second
```

```
second
```

We can use `meter` and `second` to create a variable named a and give it the value of acceleration due to gravity:

```
a = 9.8 * meter / second**2
a
```

$9.8\ meter/second^2$

The result is a *quantity* with two parts. The first is called `magnitude`:

```
a.magnitude
```

9.8

The second is called `units`:

```
a.units
```

$meter/second^2$

We can also create a quantity that represents 3.4 s

```
t = 3.4 * second
t
```

$3.4\ second$

---

and use it to compute the distance a penny would fall after t seconds with constant acceleration a:

```
a * t**2 / 2
```

$56.644\ meter$

Notice that the units of the result are correct. If we create a quantity to represent the height of the Empire State Building

```
h = 381 * meter
```

---

we can use it to compute the time the penny would take to reach the sidewalk:

```
t = sqrt(2 * h / a)
t
```

$8.817885349720552\ second$

We can also compute the velocity of the penny on impact:

```
v = a * t
v
```

```
86.41527642726142 meter/second
```

As in the previous section, the result is about 86, but now it has the correct units, m/s.

With Pint quantities, we can convert from one set of units to another, like this:

```
mile = units.mile
hour = units.hour

v.to(mile/hour)
```

```
193.30546802805432 mile/hour
```

If you are more familiar with miles per hour, this result might be easier to interpret. And it might give you a sense that this model is not realistic.

Summary

This chapter introduced a modeling framework that consists of three steps:

1.   Abstraction is the process of defining a model by deciding which elements of the real world to include and which can be left out.

2.   Analysis and simulation are ways to use a model to generate predictions, explain why things behave as they do, and design things that behave as we want.

3.   Validation is how we test whether the model is right, often by comparing predictions with measurements from the real world.

As a first example, we modeled a penny dropped from the Empire State Building, including gravity but ignoring air resistance. In the exercises, you'll have a chance to try a better model, including air resistance.

This chapter also presented Pint, a library for doing computation with units, which is convenient for converting between different units and helpful for avoiding catastrophic errors. In an ideal world, we would use Pint throughout this book to do computation with units. However, some of the libraries we'll use in later chapters can be difficult to use with Pint, especially for beginning programmers. So we won't use it after this chapter, but I hope you'll keep it in mind and find it useful in the future.

Exercises

1.1

In mathematical notation, we can write an equation like $v = at$ and it's understood that we are multiplying a and t. But that doesn't work in Python. If you put two variables side by side

```
v = a t
```

you'll get a *syntax error*, which means that something is wrong with the structure of the program. Try it out so you see what the error message looks like.

1.2

In this chapter we used the sqrt function from the NumPy library. NumPy also provides a variable named pi that contains an approximation of the mathematical constant π. We can import it like this:

```
from numpy import pi
pi
```
```
3.141592653589793
```

NumPy provides other functions we'll use, including log, exp, sin, and cos. Import sin and cos from NumPy and compute:

$$\sin^2(\pi/4) + \cos^2(\pi/4)$$

Note: A mathematical identity tells us that the answer should be 1.

1.3

Suppose you bring a 10-foot pole to the top of the Empire State Building and use it to drop the penny from h plus 10 feet.

Define a variable named foot that contains the unit foot provided by the UnitRegistry we named units. Define a variable named pole_height and give it the value 10 feet.

What happens if you add h, which is in units of meters, to pole_height, which is in units of feet? What happens if you write the addition the other way around?

```
h = 381 * meter
```

1.4

Why would it be nonsensical to add a and t? What happens if you try?

```
a = 9.8 * meter / second**2
t = 3.4 * second
```

In this example, you should get a DimensionalityError, which indicates that you have violated a rule of dimensional analysis: you cannot add quantities with different dimensions.

The error messages you get from Python are big and scary, but if you read them carefully, they contain a lot of useful information. The last line usually tells you what type of error happened, and sometimes additional information, so you might want to start from the bottom and read up.

The previous lines are a *traceback* of what was happening when the error occurred. The first section of the traceback shows the code you wrote. The following sections are often from Python libraries.

1.5

Suppose instead of dropping the penny, you throw it downward at its terminal velocity, 29 m/s. How long would it take to fall 381 m?

1.6

So far we have considered two models of a falling penny:

- If we ignore air resistance, the penny falls with constant acceleration, and we can compute the time to reach the sidewalk and the velocity of the penny when it gets there.
- If we take air resistance into account, and drop the penny at its terminal velocity, it falls with constant velocity.

Now let's consider a third model that includes elements of the first two: let's assume that the acceleration of the penny is a until the penny reaches 29 m/s, and then 0 m/s^2 afterward. What is the total time for the penny to fall 381 m?

You can break this question into three parts:

1. How long would the penny take to reach 29 m/s with constant acceleration a?
2. How far would it fall during that time?
3. How long would it take to fall the remaining distance with constant velocity 29 m/s?

I suggest you assign each intermediate result to a variable with a meaningful name. And assign units to all quantities!

```
a = 9.8 * meter / second**2
h = 381 * meter
```

1.7

When I was in high school, the pitcher on the baseball team claimed that when he threw a fastball he was throwing the ball down; that is, the ball left his hand at a downward angle. I was skeptical; watching from the side, I thought the ball left his hand at an upward angle.

Can you think of a simple model you could use to settle the argument? What factors would you include and what could you ignore? What quantities would you have to look up or estimate?

I suggest you convert all quantities to SI units like meters and seconds.

1.8

Suppose I run a 10K race in 44:52 (44 minutes and 52 seconds). What is my average pace in minutes per mile?

```
mile = units.mile
kilometer = units.kilometer
minute = units.minute
```

2

MODELING A BIKE SHARE SYSTEM

 This chapter presents a simple model of a bike share system and demonstrates the features of Python we'll use to develop simulations of real-world systems. Along the way, we'll make decisions about how to model the system. In the next chapter we'll review these decisions and gradually improve the model.

This chapter is available as a Jupyter notebook where you can read the text, run the code, and work on the exercises. You can access the notebooks at *https://allendowney.github.io/ModSimPy*.

Our Bike Share Model

Imagine a bike share system for students traveling between Olin College and Wellesley College, which are about 3 miles apart in eastern Massachusetts. Suppose the system contains 12 bikes and 2 bike racks, one at Olin and one at Wellesley, each with the capacity to hold 12 bikes.

As students arrive, check out a bike, and ride to the other campus, the number of bikes in each location changes. In the simulation, we'll need to keep track of where the bikes are. To do that, we'll use a function called State, which is defined in the ModSim library:

```
bikeshare = State(olin=10, wellesley=2)
```

The equations in parentheses create two variables, olin and wellesley, and give them the values 10 and 2.

The State function stores these variables and their values in a State object, which gets assigned to a new variable named bikeshare. Variables stored inside a State object are called *state variables*.

In this example, the state variables represent the number of bikes at each location. Their values indicate that there are 10 bikes at Olin and 2 at Wellesley.

We can get the value of a state variable using the *dot operator*, like this:

```
bikeshare.olin
```

```
10
```

and this:

```
bikeshare.wellesley
```

```
2
```

To display all of the state variables and their values, you can enter just the name of the object:

```
bikeshare
```

	state
olin	10
wellesley	2

These values make up the *state* of the system.

We can update the state by assigning new values to the variables. For example, if a student moves a bike from Olin to Wellesley, we can figure out the new values and assign them:

```
bikeshare.olin = 9
bikeshare.wellesley = 3
```

We can also use *update operators*, -= and +=, to subtract 1 from olin and add 1 to wellesley:

```
bikeshare.olin -= 1
bikeshare.wellesley += 1
```

The result is the same either way.

Defining Functions

So far we have used functions defined in NumPy and the ModSim library. Now we're going to define our own functions.

When you are developing code in Jupyter, it is often efficient to write a few lines of code, test them to confirm they do what you intend, and then use them to define a new function. For example, these lines move a bike from Olin to Wellesley:

```
bikeshare.olin -= 1
bikeshare.wellesley += 1
```

Rather than repeat them every time a bike moves, we can define a new function:

```
def bike_to_wellesley():
    bikeshare.olin -= 1
    bikeshare.wellesley += 1
```

def is a special word in Python that indicates we are defining a new function. The name of the function is bike_to_wellesley. The empty parentheses indicate that this function requires no additional information when it runs. The colon indicates the beginning of an indented *code block*.

The next two lines are the *body* of the function. They have to be indented; by convention, the indentation is four spaces.

When you define a function, it has no immediate effect. The body of the function doesn't run until you *call* the function. Here's how to call this function:

```
bike_to_wellesley()
```

When you call the function, it runs the code in the body, which updates the variables of the bikeshare object; you can check by displaying the new state:

```
show(bikeshare)
```

	state
olin	6
wellesley	6

When you call a function, you have to include the parentheses. If you leave them out, you get this:

```
bike_to_wellesley
```

```
<function __main__.bike_to_wellesley()>
```

This result indicates that bike_to_wellesley is a function. You don't have to know what __main__ means, but if you see something like this, it probably means that you named a function but didn't actually call it. So don't forget the parentheses.

Print Statements

As you write more complicated programs, it is easy to lose track of what is going on. One of the most useful tools for debugging is the *print statement*, which displays text in the Jupyter notebook.

Normally when Jupyter runs the code in a cell, it displays the value of the last line of code. For example, if you run

```
bikeshare.olin
bikeshare.wellesley
```
```
6
```

Jupyter runs both lines, but it only displays the value of the second. If you want to display more than one value, you can use print statements:

```
print(bikeshare.olin)
print(bikeshare.wellesley)
```
```
6
6
```

When you call the print function, you can put a variable in parentheses, as in the previous example, or you can provide a sequence of variables separated by commas, like this:

```
print(bikeshare.olin, bikeshare.wellesley)
```
```
6 6
```

Python looks up the values of the variables and displays them; in this example, it displays two values on the same line, with a space between them.

Print statements are useful for debugging functions. For example, we can add a print statement to bike_to_wellesley, like this:

```
def bike_to_wellesley():
    print('Moving a bike to Wellesley')
    bikeshare.olin -= 1
    bikeshare.wellesley += 1
```

Each time we call this version of the function, it displays a message, which can help us keep track of what the program is doing. The message in this example is a *string*, which is a sequence of letters and other symbols in quotes.

Just like bike_to_wellesley, we can define a function that moves a bike from Wellesley to Olin:

```
def bike_to_olin():
    print('Moving a bike to Olin')
    bikeshare.wellesley -= 1
    bikeshare.olin += 1
```

And we can call it like this:

```
bike_to_olin()
```

Moving a bike to Olin

One benefit of defining functions is that you avoid repeating chunks of code, which makes programs smaller. Another benefit is that the name you give the function documents what it does, which makes programs more readable.

if Statements

At this point we have functions that simulate moving bikes; now let's think about simulating customers. As a simple model of customer behavior, I will use a random number generator to determine when customers arrive at each station.

The ModSim library provides a function called flip that generates random "coin tosses." When you call it, you provide a probability between 0 and 1, like this:

```
flip(0.7)
```

True

The result is one of two values: True with probability 0.7 (in this example) or False with probability 0.3. If you run flip like this 100 times, you should get True about 70 times and False about 30 times. But the results are random, so they might differ from these expectations.

True and False are special values defined by Python. They are called *Boolean* values because they are related to Boolean algebra (we won't cover Boolean algebra in this book, but I encourage you to explore it on your own). Note that they are not strings. There is a difference between True, which is a Boolean value, and 'True', which is a string.

We can use Boolean values to control the behavior of the program, using an if statement:

```
if flip(0.5):
    print('heads')
```

If the result from flip is True, the program displays the string heads. Otherwise, it does nothing.

The syntax for if statements is similar to the syntax for function definitions: the first line has to end with a colon, and the lines inside the if statement have to be indented.

Optionally, you can add an else clause to indicate what should happen if the result is False:

```
if flip(0.5):
    print('heads')
else:
    print('tails')
```

```
heads
```

If you run the previous code a few times, it should print heads about half the time, and tails about half the time.

Now we can use flip to simulate the arrival of customers who want to borrow a bike. Suppose students arrive at the Olin station every two minutes on average. In that case, the chance of an arrival during any one-minute period is 50 percent, and we can simulate it like this:

```
if flip(0.5):
    bike_to_wellesley()
```

```
Moving a bike to Wellesley
```

If students arrive at the Wellesley station every three minutes, on average, the chance of an arrival during any one-minute period is 33 percent, and we can simulate it like this:

```
if flip(0.33):
    bike_to_olin()
```

We can combine these snippets into a function that simulates a *time step*, which is an interval of time, in this case one minute:

```
def step():
    if flip(0.5):
        bike_to_wellesley()

    if flip(0.33):
        bike_to_olin()
```

Then we can simulate a time step like this:

```
step()
```

Depending on the results from flip, this function might move a bike to Olin, or to Wellesley, or neither, or both.

Parameters

The previous version of step is fine if the arrival probabilities never change, but in reality they vary over time. So instead of putting the constant values 0.5 and 0.33 in step, we can replace them with *parameters*. Parameters are variables whose values are set when a function is called.

Here's a version of step that takes two parameters, p1 and p2:

```
def step(p1, p2):
    if flip(p1):
        bike_to_wellesley()

    if flip(p2):
        bike_to_olin()
```

The values of p1 and p2 are not set inside this function; instead, they are provided when the function is called, like this:

```
step(0.5, 0.33)
```

```
Moving a bike to Olin
```

The values you provide when you call the function are called *arguments*. The arguments, 0.5 and 0.33 in this example, get assigned to the parameters, p1 and p2, in order. So running this function has the same effect as:

```
p1 = 0.5
p2 = 0.33

if flip(p1):
    bike_to_wellesley()

if flip(p2):
    bike_to_olin()
```

```
Moving a bike to Wellesley
```

The advantage of using parameters is that you can call the same function many times, providing different arguments each time.

Adding parameters to a function is called *generalization*, because it makes the function more general; without parameters, the function always does the same thing; with parameters, it can do a range of things.

for Loops

At some point you will get sick of running the same code over and over. Fortunately, there is an easy way to repeat a chunk of code, the for loop. Here's an example:

```
for i in range(3):
    print(i)
    bike_to_wellesley()
```

```
0
Moving a bike to Wellesley
1
Moving a bike to Wellesley
2
Moving a bike to Wellesley
```

The syntax here should look familiar; the first line ends with a colon, and the lines inside the for loop are indented. The other elements of the loop are the following:

- The words for and in are special words we have to use in a for loop.
- range is a Python function we use to control the number of times the loop runs.
- i is a *loop variable* that gets created when the for loop runs.

When this loop runs, it runs the code inside the loop three times. The first time, the value of i is 0; the second time, it is 1; the third time, it is 2. Each time through the loop, it prints the value of i and moves one bike to Wellesley.

TimeSeries

When we run a simulation, we often want to save the results for later analysis. The ModSim library provides a TimeSeries object for this purpose. A TimeSeries contains a sequence of timestamps and a corresponding sequence of quantities. A *timestamp* is a value that specifies a point in time. In this example, the timestamps are integers representing minutes and the quantities are the number of bikes at one location.

Since we have moved a number of bikes around, let's start again with a new State object:

```
bikeshare = State(olin=10, wellesley=2)
```

We can create a new, empty `TimeSeries` like this:

```
results = TimeSeries()
```

And we can add a quantity like this:

```
results[0] = bikeshare.olin
```

The number in square brackets is the timestamp, also called a *label*.

We can use a `TimeSeries` inside a `for` loop to store the results of the simulation:

```
for i in range(3):
    print(i)
    step(0.6, 0.6)
    results[i+1] = bikeshare.olin
```
```
0
Moving a bike to Wellesley
1
Moving a bike to Olin
2
Moving a bike to Olin
```

Each time through the loop, we print the value of i and call step, which updates bikeshare. Then we store the number of bikes at Olin in results. We use the loop variable, i, to compute the timestamp, i+1.

The first time through the loop, the value of i is 0, so the timestamp is 1. The last time, the value of i is 2, so the timestamp is 3. When the loop exits, results contains four timestamps, from 0 through 3, and the number of bikes at Olin at the end of each time step.

We can display the `TimeSeries` like this:

```
show(results)
```

Time	Quantity
0	10
1	9
2	10
3	11

The left column is the timestamps; the right column is the quantities.

Plotting

results provides a function called plot that we can use to plot the results, and the ModSim library provides decorate, which we can use to label the axes and give the figure a title:

```
results.plot()

decorate(title='Olin-Wellesley bikeshare',
         xlabel='Time step (min)',
         ylabel='Number of bikes')
```

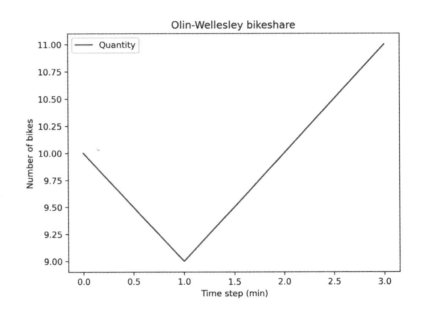

The result should be a plot with time on the x-axis and the number of bikes on the y-axis. Since we only ran three time steps, it might not be very interesting.

Summary

This chapter introduced the tools we need to run simulations, record the results, and plot them.

We used a State object to represent the state of the system. Then we used the flip function and an if statement to simulate a single time step. We used a for loop to simulate a series of steps, and a TimeSeries to record the results. Finally, we used plot and decorate to plot the results.

In the next chapter, we will extend this simulation to make it a little more realistic.

Exercises

2.1

What happens if you spell the name of a state variable wrong? Edit the following code, change the spelling of wellesley, and run it:

```
bikeshare = State(olin=10, wellesley=2)

bikeshare.wellesley
```

```
2
```

The error message uses the word *attribute*, which is another name for what we are calling a state variable.

2.2

Make a State object with a third state variable, called downtown, with initial value 0, and display the state of the system.

2.3

Wrap the code in the chapter in a function named run_simulation that takes three parameters, named p1, p2, and num_steps.

It should:

1. Create a TimeSeries object to hold the results.
2. Use a for loop to run step the number of times specified by num_steps, passing along the specified values of p1 and p2.
3. After each step, it should save the number of bikes at Olin in the TimeSeries.
4. After the for loop, it should plot the results and decorate the axes.

To test your function:

1. Create a State object with the initial state of the system.
2. Call run_simulation with parameters p1=0.3, p2=0.2, and num_steps=60.

Under the Hood

This optional section contains additional information about the functions we've used and pointers to their documentation.

State and TimeSeries objects are based on the Series object defined by the pandas library. The documentation is at *https://pandas.pydata.org/pandas -docs/stable/reference/api/pandas.Series.html*.

Series objects provide their own plot function, which is why we call it like this:

```
results.plot()
```

instead of like this:

```
plot(results)
```

You can read the documentation of `Series.plot` at *https://pandas.pydata.org/pandas-docs/stable/reference/api/pandas.Series.plot.html*.

`decorate` is based on Matplotlib, which is a widely used plotting library for Python. Matplotlib provides separate functions for `title`, `xlabel`, and `ylabel`. `decorate` makes them a little easier to use. For the list of arguments you can pass to decorate, see *https://matplotlib.org/3.2.2/api/axes_api.html?highlight=axes#module-matplotlib.axes*.

The `flip` function uses NumPy's `random` function to generate a random number between 0 and 1, then returns `True` or `False` with the given probability. You can get the source code for `flip` (or any other function) by running the following code:

```
source_code(flip)
```

```
def flip(p=0.5):
    """Flips a coin with the given probability.

    p: float 0-1

    returns: boolean (True or False)
    """
    return np.random.random() < p
```

3

ITERATIVE MODELING

To paraphrase two Georges, "All models are wrong, but some models are more wrong than others." This chapter demonstrates the process we use to make models less wrong. As an example, we'll review the bike share model from the previous chapter, consider its strengths and weaknesses, and gradually improve it. We'll also see ways to use the model to understand the behavior of the system and evaluate designs intended to make it work better.

This chapter is available as a Jupyter notebook where you can read the text, run the code, and work on the exercises. You can access the notebooks at *https://allendowney.github.io/ModSimPy*.

Iterating on Our Bike Share Model

The model we have so far is simple, but it is based on unrealistic assumptions. Before you go on, take a minute to review the model from the previous chapter. What assumptions is it based on? Make a list of ways this model might be unrealistic; that is, what are the differences between the model and the real world?

Here are some of the differences on my list:

- In the model, a student is equally likely to arrive during any one-minute period. In reality, this probability varies depending on time of day, day of the week, and so on.

- The model does not account for travel time from one bike station to another.

- The model does not check whether a bike is available, so it's possible for the number of bikes to be negative (as you might have noticed in some of your simulations).

Some of these modeling decisions are better than others. For example, the first assumption might be reasonable if we simulate the system for a short period of time, like one hour. The second assumption is not very realistic, but it might not affect the results very much, depending on what we use the model for. On the other hand, the third assumption seems more problematic. It is relatively easy to fix, though; in this chapter, we'll fix it.

This process, starting with a simple model, identifying the most important problems, and making gradual improvements, is called *iterative modeling*. For any physical system, there are many possible models, based on different assumptions and simplifications. It often takes several iterations to develop a model that is good enough for the intended purpose, but no more complicated than necessary.

Using More Than One State Object

Before we go on, let's make a few changes to the code from the previous chapter. First we'll generalize the functions we wrote so they take a State object as a parameter. Then, we'll make the code more readable by adding documentation.

Here's one of the functions from the previous chapter, bike_to_wellesley:

```
def bike_to_wellesley():
    bikeshare.olin -= 1
    bikeshare.wellesley += 1
```

When this function is called, it modifies bikeshare. As long as there is only one State object, that's fine, but what if there is more than one bike share system in the world? Or what if we want to run more than one simulation?

This function would be more flexible if it took a State object as a parameter. Here's what that looks like:

```
def bike_to_wellesley(state):
    state.olin -= 1
    state.wellesley += 1
```

The name of the parameter is state, rather than bikeshare, as a reminder that the value of state could be any State object, not just the one we called bikeshare.

This version of bike_to_wellesley requires a State object as a parameter, so we have to provide one when we call it:

```
bikeshare = State(olin=10, wellesley=2)
bike_to_wellesley(bikeshare)
```

Again, the argument we provide gets assigned to the parameter, so this function call has the same effect as:

```
state = bikeshare
state.olin -= 1
state.wellesley += 1
```

Now we can create as many State objects as we want:

```
bikeshare1 = State(olin=10, wellesley=2)
bikeshare2 = State(olin=2, wellesley=10)
```

and update them independently:

```
bike_to_wellesley(bikeshare1)
bike_to_wellesley(bikeshare2)
```

Changes in bikeshare1 do not affect bikeshare2, and vice versa. So we can simulate different bike share systems or run multiple simulations of the same system.

Documentation

Another problem with the code we have so far is that it contains no *documentation*. Documentation is text we add to a program to help other programmers read and understand it. It has no effect on the program when it runs.

There are two kinds of documentation. A *docstring* is a string in triple quotes that appears at the beginning of a function. A *comment* is a line of text that begins with a hash mark, #.

Here's a version of bike_to_olin with a docstring and a comment:

```
def bike_to_olin(state):
    """Move one bike from Wellesley to Olin

    state: bikeshare State object
    """
    # We decrease one state variable and increase the
    # other so the total number of bikes is unchanged.
    state.wellesley -= 1
    state.olin += 1
```

Docstrings follow a conventional format: the first line is a single sentence that describes what the function does, and the following lines explain what the parameters are. A function's docstring should include the information someone needs to know to *use* the function; it should not include details about how the function works.

Comments provide details about how the function works, especially if there is something that would not be obvious to someone reading the program.

Dealing with Negative Bikes

The changes we've made so far improve the quality of the code, but we haven't done anything yet to improve the quality of the model. Let's do that now.

Currently the simulation does not check whether a bike is available when a customer arrives, so the number of bikes at a location can be negative. That's not very realistic. Here's a version of bike_to_olin that fixes the problem:

```
def bike_to_olin(state):
    if state.wellesley == 0:
        return
    state.wellesley -= 1
    state.olin += 1
```

The first line checks whether the number of bikes at Wellesley is zero. If so, it uses a *return statement*, which causes the function to end immediately, without running the rest of the statements. So if there are no bikes at Wellesley, we return from bike_to_olin without changing the state.

We can test it by initializing the state with no bikes at Wellesley and calling bike_to_olin:

```
bikeshare = State(olin=12, wellesley=0)
bike_to_olin(bikeshare)
```

The state of the system should be unchanged.

```
show(bikeshare)
```
----

	state
olin	12
wellesley	0

No more negative bikes (at least at Wellesley).

Comparison Operators

The updated version of bike_to_olin uses the equals operator, ==, which compares two values and returns True if they are equal, and False otherwise.

It is easy to confuse the equals operator with the assignment operator, =, which assigns a value to a variable. For example, the following statement creates a variable, x, if it doesn't already exist, and gives it the value 5:

```
x = 5
```

On the other hand, the following statement checks whether x is 5 and returns True or False:

```
x == 5
```
```
True
```

It does not create x or change its value.

You can use the equals operator in an if statement, like this:

```
if x == 5:
    print('yes, x is 5')
```
```
yes, x is 5
```

If you make a mistake and use = in an if statement, like this:

```
if x = 5:
    print('yes, x is 5')
```

that's a *syntax error*, which means that the structure of the program is invalid. Python will print an error message and the program won't run.

The equals operator is one of Python's *comparison operators*; the complete list is in Table 3-1.

Table 3-1: A List of Comparison Operators

Operation	Symbol
Less than	<
Greater than	>
Less than or equal	<=
Greater than or equal	>=
Equal	==
Not equal	!=

Now let's get back to the bike share system.

Introducing Metrics

At this point we have the ability to simulate the behavior of the system. Since the arrival of customers is random, the state of the system is different each time we run a simulation. Models like this are called random or *stochastic*; models that do the same thing every time they run are *deterministic*.

Suppose we want to use our model to predict how well the bike share system will work or to design a system that works better. First, we have to decide what we mean by "how well" and "better."

From the customer's point of view, we might like to know the probability of finding an available bike. From the system owner's point of view, we might want to minimize the number of customers who don't get a bike when they want one or maximize the number of bikes in use. Statistics like these that quantify how well the system works are called *metrics*.

As an example, let's measure the number of unhappy customers. Here's a version of bike_to_olin that keeps track of the number of customers who arrive at a station with no bikes:

```
def bike_to_olin(state):
    if state.wellesley == 0:
        state.wellesley_empty += 1
        return
    state.wellesley -= 1
    state.olin += 1
```

If a customer arrives at the Wellesley station and finds no bike available, bike_to_olin updates wellesley_empty, which counts the number of unhappy customers.

This function only works if we initialize wellesley_empty when we create the State object, like this:

```
bikeshare = State(olin=12, wellesley=0,
                  wellesley_empty=0)
```

We can test it by calling bike_to_olin:

```
bike_to_olin(bikeshare)
```

After this update, there should be 12 bikes at Olin, no bikes at Wellesley, and one unhappy customer:

```
show(bikeshare)
```

	state
olin	12
wellesley	0
wellesley_empty	1

Looks good!

Summary

In this chapter, we wrote several versions of bike_to_olin:

- We added a parameter, state, so we can work with more than one State object.

- We added a docstring that explains how to use the function and a comment that explains how it works.

- We used a conditional operator, ==, to check whether a bike is available, in order to avoid negative bikes.

- We added a state variable, wellesley_empty, to count the number of unhappy customers, which is a metric we'll use to quantify how well the system works.

In the exercises, you'll update bike_to_wellesley the same way and test it by running a simulation.

Exercises

3.1

Modify bike_to_wellesley so it checks whether a bike is available at Olin. If not, it should add 1 to olin_empty.

To test it, create a State object that initializes olin and olin_empty to 0, run bike_to_wellesley, and check the result.

3.2

Now run the simulation with parameters p1=0.3, p2=0.2, and num_steps=60, and confirm that the number of bikes is never negative.

Start with this initial state:

```
bikeshare = State(olin=10, wellesley=2,
                  olin_empty=0, wellesley_empty=0)
```

4

PARAMETERS AND METRICS

In the previous chapter we defined metrics that quantify the performance of a bike sharing system. In this chapter we'll see how those metrics depend on the parameters of the system, like the arrival rate of customers at the stations. I will also present a program development strategy, called incremental development, that might help you write programs faster and spend less time debugging.

This chapter is available as a Jupyter notebook where you can read the text, run the code, and work on the exercises. You can access the notebooks at *https://allendowney.github.io/ModSimPy*.

Functions That Return Values

We have used several functions that return values. For example, when you run sqrt, it returns a number you can assign to a variable:

```
from numpy import sqrt

root_2 = sqrt(2)
root_2
```

```
1.4142135623730951
```

When you run State, it returns a new State object:

```
bikeshare = State(olin=10, wellesley=2)
bikeshare
```

	state
olin	10
wellesley	2

Not all functions have return values. For example, when you run step, it updates a State object, but it doesn't return a value.

To write functions that return values, we can use a return statement:

```
def add_five(x):
    return x + 5
```

add_five takes a parameter, x, which could be any number. It computes x + 5 and returns the result. So if we run it like this, the result is 8:

```
add_five(3)
```

```
8
```

As a more useful example, here's a version of run_simulation that creates a State object, runs a simulation, and then returns the State object:

```
def run_simulation(p1, p2, num_steps):
    state = State(olin=10, wellesley=2,
                  olin_empty=0, wellesley_empty=0)

    for i in range(num_steps):
        step(state, p1, p2)

    return state
```

We can call run_simulation like this:

```
final_state = run_simulation(0.3, 0.2, 60)
```

The result is a State object that represents the final state of the system, including the metrics we'll use to evaluate the performance of the system:

```
print(final_state.olin_empty,
    final_state.wellesley_empty)
```

```
0 0
```

The simulation we just ran starts with olin=10 and wellesley=2 and uses the values p1=0.3, p2=0.2, and num_steps=60. These five values are *parameters of the model*, which are quantities that determine the behavior of the system.

It is easy to get the parameters of a model confused with the parameters of a function. It is especially easy because the parameters of a model often appear as parameters of a function. For example, the previous version of run_simulation takes p1, p2, and num_steps as parameters. So we can call run_simulation with different parameters and see how the metrics, like the number of unhappy customers, depend on the parameters. But before we do that, we need a new version of a for loop.

Loops and Arrays

In run_simulation, we use this for loop:

```
for i in range(num_steps):
    step(state, p1, p2)
```

In this example, range creates a sequence of numbers from 0 to num_steps (including 0 but not num_steps). Each time through the loop, the next number in the sequence gets assigned to the loop variable, i.

But range only works with integers; to get a sequence of noninteger values, we can use linspace, which is provided by NumPy:

```
from numpy import linspace

p1_array = linspace(0, 1, 5)
p1_array
```
```
array([0. , 0.25, 0.5 , 0.75, 1. ])
```

The arguments indicate where the sequence should start and stop, and how many elements it should contain. In this example, the sequence contains 5 equally spaced numbers, starting at 0 and ending at 1. The result is a NumPy *array*, which is a new kind of object we have not seen before. An array is a container for a sequence of numbers.

We can use an array in a for loop like this:

```
for p1 in p1_array:
    print(p1)
```
```
0.0
0.25
0.5
0.75
1.0
```

When this loop runs, it does the following:

1. Gets the first value from the array and assigns it to p1
2. Runs the body of the loop, which prints p1
3. Gets the next value from the array and assigns it to p1
4. Runs the body of the loop, which prints p1

The loop does this until it gets to the end of the array. This will come in handy in the next section.

Sweeping Parameters

If we know the actual values of parameters like p1 and p2, we can use them to make specific predictions, like how many bikes will be at Olin after one hour.

But prediction is not the only goal; models like this are also used to explain why systems behave as they do and to evaluate alternative designs. For example, if we observe the system and notice that we often run out of bikes at a particular time, we could use the model to figure out why that happens. And if we are considering adding more bikes, or another station, we could evaluate the effect of various "what if" scenarios.

As an example, suppose we have enough data to estimate that p2 is about 0.2, but we don't have any information about p1. We could run simulations with a range of values for p1 and see how the results vary. This process is called *sweeping* a parameter, in the sense that the value of the parameter "sweeps" through a range of possible values.

Now that we know about loops and arrays, we can use them like this:

```
p1_array = linspace(0, 0.6, 6)
p2 = 0.2
num_steps = 60

for p1 in p1_array:
    final_state = run_simulation(p1, p2, num_steps)
    print(p1, final_state.olin_empty)
```
```
0.0 0
0.12 0
0.24 0
0.36 3
0.48 14
0.6 11
```

Each time through the loop, we run a simulation with a different value of p1 and the same value of p2, 0.2. Then we print p1 and the number of unhappy customers at Olin.

To save and plot the results, we can use a SweepSeries object, which is similar to a TimeSeries; the difference is that the labels in a SweepSeries are parameter values rather than time values.

We can create an empty SweepSeries like this:

```
sweep = SweepSeries()
```

and add values like this:

```
p1_array = linspace(0, 0.6, 31)

for p1 in p1_array:
    final_state = run_simulation(p1, p2, num_steps)
    sweep[p1] = final_state.olin_empty
```

The result is a SweepSeries that maps from each value of p1 to the resulting number of unhappy customers.

We can plot the elements of the SweepSeries like this:

```
sweep.plot(label='Olin', color='C1')

decorate(title='Olin-Wellesley bikeshare',
         xlabel='Customer rate at Olin (p1 in customers/min)',
         ylabel='Number of unhappy customers at Olin')
```

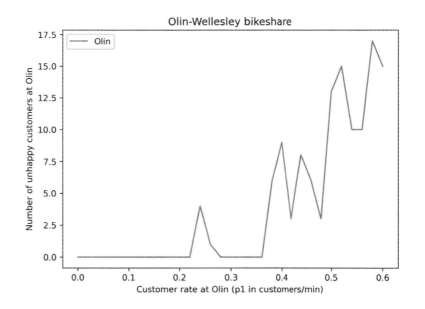

The argument color='C1' specifies the color of the line (which you won't be able to see in the printed version of this book). The TimeSeries we have plotted so far use the default color, C0, which is blue. I use a different color for SweepSeries to remind us that it is not a TimeSeries.

When the arrival rate at Olin is low, there are plenty of bikes and no unhappy customers. As the arrival rate increases, we are more likely to run out of bikes, and the number of unhappy customers increases. The line is jagged because the simulation is based on random numbers. Sometimes we get lucky and there are relatively few unhappy customers; other times we are unlucky and there are more.

Incremental Development

When you start writing programs that are more than a few lines, you might find yourself spending more time debugging. The more code you write before you start debugging, the harder it is to find the problem.

Incremental development is a way of programming that tries to minimize the pain of debugging. The fundamental steps are the following:

1. Always start with a working program. If you have an example from a book, or a program you wrote that is similar to what you are working on, start with that. Otherwise, start with something you *know* is correct, like x = 5. Run the program and confirm that it does what you expect.

2. Make one small, testable change at a time. A "testable" change is one that displays something or has some other effect you can check. Ideally, you should know what the correct answer is or be able to check it by performing another computation.

3. Run the program and see if the change worked. If so, go back to Step 2. If not, you have to do some debugging, but if the change you made was small, it shouldn't take long to find the problem.

When this process works, your changes usually work the first time or, if they don't, the problem is obvious. In practice, there are two problems with incremental development:

- Sometimes you have to write extra code to generate visible output that you can check. This extra code is called *scaffolding* because you use it to build the program and then remove it when you are done. That might seem like a waste, but time you spend on scaffolding is almost always time you save on debugging.

- When you are getting started, it might not be obvious how to choose the steps that get from x = 5 to the program you are trying to write. You will see more examples of this process as we go along, and you will get better with experience.

If you find yourself writing more than a few lines of code before you start testing, and you are spending a lot of time debugging, try incremental development.

Summary

This chapter introduced functions that return values, which we used to write a version of run_simulation that returns a State object with the final state of the system. It also introduced linspace, which we used to create a NumPy array, and SweepSeries, which we used to store the results of a parameter sweep. We used a parameter sweep to explore the relationship between one of the parameters, p1, and the number of unhappy customers, which is a metric that quantifies how well (or badly) the system works. In the exercises, you'll have a chance to sweep other parameters and compute other metrics.

In the next chapter, we'll move on to a new problem, modeling and predicting world population growth.

Exercises

4.1

Write a function called make_state that creates a State object with the state variables olin=10 and wellesley=2 and then returns the new State object. Then write a line of code that calls make_state and assigns the result to a variable named init.

4.2

Read the documentation of linspace at *https://numpy.org/doc/stable/ reference/generated/numpy.linspace.html*. Then use it to make an array of 101 equally spaced points between 0 and 1 (including both).

4.3

Wrap the code from this chapter in a function named sweep_p1 that takes an array called p1_array as a parameter. It should create a new SweepSeries and run a simulation for each value of p1 in p1_array, with p2=0.2 and num_steps=60. It should store the results in the SweepSeries and return it.

Use your function to generate a SweepSeries and then plot the number of unhappy customers at Olin as a function of p1. Label the axes.

4.4

Write a function called sweep_p2 that runs simulations with p1=0.5 and a range of values for p2. It should store the results in a SweepSeries and return the SweepSeries.

Challenge Exercises

The following two exercises are a little more challenging. If you are comfortable with what you have learned so far, you should give them a try. If you feel like you have your hands full, you might want to skip them for now.

4.5

Because our simulations are random, the results vary from one run to another, and the results of a parameter sweep tend to be noisy. We can get a clearer picture of the relationship between a parameter and a metric by running multiple simulations with the same parameter and taking the average of the results.

Write a function called run_multiple_simulations that takes as parameters p1, p2, num_steps, and num_runs. num_runs specifies how many times it should call run_simulation. After each run, it should store the total number of unhappy customers (at Olin or Wellesley) in a TimeSeries. At the end, it should return the TimeSeries.

Test your function with these parameters:

```
p1 = 0.3
p2 = 0.3
num_steps = 60
num_runs = 10
```

Display the resulting TimeSeries and use the mean function from NumPy to compute the average number of unhappy customers.

4.6

Continuing the previous exercise, use run_multiple_simulations to run simulations with a range of values for p1 and p2:

```
p2 = 0.3
num_steps = 60
num_runs = 20
```

Store the results in a SweepSeries, then plot the average number of unhappy customers as a function of p1. Label the axes.

What value of p1 minimizes the average number of unhappy customers?

Under the Hood

The object you get when you call SweepSeries is actually a pandas Series, the same as the object you get from TimeSeries. I give them different names to help us remember that they play different roles.

Series provides a number of functions, which you can read about at *https://pandas.pydata.org/pandas-docs/stable/reference/api/pandas.Series.html*. They include mean, which computes the average of the values in the Series, so if you have a Series named totals, for example, you can compute the mean like this:

```
totals.mean()
```

Series provides other statistical functions, like std, which computes the standard deviation of the values in the series.

In this chapter I use the argument color to specify the color of a line plot. You can read about other colors defined by Matplotlib at *https://matplotlib.org/3.3.2/tutorials/colors/colors.html*.

5

BUILDING A POPULATION MODEL

 In 1968 Paul Erlich published *The Population Bomb*, in which he predicted that world population would grow quickly during the 1970s, that agricultural production could not keep up, and that mass starvation in the next two decades was inevitable. As someone who grew up during those decades, I am happy to report that those predictions were wrong. But world population growth is still a topic of concern, and it is an open question how many people Earth can sustain while maintaining and improving our quality of life.

In this chapter and the next, we'll use tools from the previous chapters to model world population growth since 1950 and generate predictions for the next 50–100 years. For background on world population growth, watch this video from the American Museum of Natural History: *https://www.youtube.com/watch?v=PUwmA3Q0_OE*.

This chapter is available as a Jupyter notebook where you can read the text, run the code, and work on the exercise. You can access the notebooks at *https://allendowney.github.io/ModSimPy*.

Exploring the Data

The Wikipedia article on world population contains tables with estimates of world population from prehistory to the present and projections for the future (*https://en.wikipedia.org/wiki/Estimates_of_historical_world_population*). To read this data, we will use the pandas library, which provides functions for working with data. The function we'll use is read_html, which can read a web page and extract data from any tables it contains. Before we can use it, we have to import it:

```
from pandas import read_html
```

Now we can use it like this:

```
filename = 'World_population_estimates.html'
tables = read_html(filename,
                   header=0,
                   index_col=0,
                   decimal='M')
```

The arguments are the following:

filename   The name of the file (including the directory it's in) as a string. This argument can also be a URL starting with http.

header   Indicates which row of each table should be considered the *header*, that is, the set of labels that identify the columns. In this case it is the first row (numbered 0).

index_col   Indicates which column of each table should be considered the *index*, that is, the set of labels that identify the rows. In this case it is the first column, which contains the years.

decimal   Normally this argument is used to indicate which character should be considered a decimal point, because some conventions use a period and some use a comma. In this case I am abusing the feature by treating M as a decimal point, which allows the estimates that are expressed in millions (M) to be read as numbers.

The result, which is assigned to tables, is a sequence that contains one DataFrame for each table. A DataFrame is an object, defined by pandas, that represents tabular data.

To select a DataFrame from tables, we can use the bracket operator:

```
table2 = tables[2]
```

This line selects the third table (numbered 2), which contains population estimates from 1950 to 2016.

We can use head to display the first few rows of the table (here we also show only the first few columns):

```
table2.head()
```

Year	United States Census Bureau (2017)[28]	Population Reference Bureau (1973–2016)[15]
1950	2557628654	2.516000e+09
1951	2594939877	NaN
1952	2636772306	NaN
1953	2682053389	NaN
1954	2730228104	NaN

The first column, which is labeled Year, is special. It is the *index* for this DataFrame, which means it contains the labels for the rows. Notice some of the values use scientific notation; for example, 2.516000e+09 is shorthand for $2.516 \cdot 10^9$ or 2.544 billion. The table also contains instances of NaN, which is a special value that indicates missing data.

The column labels are long strings, which makes them hard to work with. We can replace them with shorter strings like this:

```
table2.columns = ['census', 'prb', 'un', 'maddison',
                  'hyde', 'tanton', 'biraben', 'mj',
                  'thomlinson', 'durand', 'clark']
```

Now we can select a column from the DataFrame using the dot operator, like selecting a state variable from a State object.

Here are the estimates from the United States Census Bureau:

```
census = table2.census / 1e9
```

The result is a pandas Series, which is similar to the TimeSeries and SweepSeries objects we've been using.

The number 1e9 is a shorter way to write 1000000000 or one billion. When we divide a Series by a number, it divides all of the elements of the Series. From here on, we'll express population estimates in terms of billions.

We can use tail to see the last few elements of the Series:

```
census.tail()
```

Year	census
2012	7.013871
2013	7.092128
2014	7.169968
2015	7.247893
2016	7.325997

The left column is the *index* of the Series; in this example, it contains the dates. The right column contains the *values*, which are population estimates. In 2016 the world population was about 7.3 billion.

Here are the estimates from the United Nations Department of Economic and Social Affairs (UN DESA):

```
un = table2.un / 1e9
un.tail()
```

Year	un
2012	7.080072
2013	7.162119
2014	7.243784
2015	7.349472
2016	NaN

The most recent estimate we have from the UN is for 2015, so the value for 2016 is NaN.

Now we can plot the estimates like this:

```
def plot_estimates():
    census.plot(style=':', label='US Census')
    un.plot(style='--', label='UN DESA')
    decorate(xlabel='Year',
             ylabel='World population (billions)')
```

The keyword argument style=':' specifies a dotted line; style='--' specifies a dashed line. The label argument provides the string that appears in the legend. Here's what it looks like:

```
plot_estimates()
decorate(title='World population estimates')
```

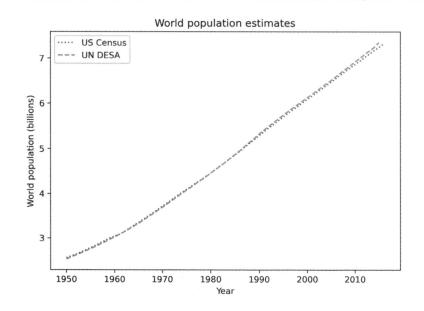

The lines overlap almost completely, but the most recent estimates diverge slightly. In the next section, we'll quantify these differences.

Absolute and Relative Errors

Estimates of world population from the US Census and the UN DESA differ slightly. One way to characterize this difference is *absolute error*, which is the absolute value of the difference between the estimates.

To compute absolute errors, we can import abs from NumPy:

```
from numpy import abs
```

and use it like this:

```
abs_error = abs(un - census)
abs_error.tail()
```

Year	0
2012	0.066201
2013	0.069991
2014	0.073816
2015	0.101579
2016	NaN

When you subtract two Series objects, the result is a new Series. Because one of the estimates for 2016 is NaN, the result for 2016 is NaN.

To summarize the results, we can compute the *mean absolute error*:

```
from numpy import mean

mean(abs_error)
```

```
0.029034508242424265
```

On average, the estimates differ by about 0.029 billion. But we can also use max to compute the *maximum absolute error*:

```
from numpy import max

max(abs_error)
```

```
0.10157921199999986
```

In the worst case, they differ by about 0.1 billion. Now 0.1 billion is a lot of people, so that might sound like a serious discrepancy. But counting everyone in the world is hard, and we should not expect the estimates to be exact.

Another way to quantify the magnitude of the difference is *relative error*, which is the size of the error divided by the estimates themselves:

```
rel_error = 100 * abs_error / census
rel_error.tail()
```

Year	0
2012	0.943860
2013	0.986888
2014	1.029514
2015	1.401500
2016	NaN

I multiplied by 100 so we can interpret the results as a percentage. In 2015, the difference between the estimates is about 1.4 percent, and that happens to be the maximum.

Again, we can summarize the results by computing the mean:

```
mean(rel_error)
```

```
0.5946585816022846
```

The mean relative error is about 0.6 percent. So that's not bad.

You might wonder why I divided by census rather than un. In general, if you think one estimate is better than the other, you put the better one in the denominator. In this case, I don't know which is better, so I put the smaller one in the denominator, which makes the computed errors a little bigger.

Modeling Population Growth

Suppose we want to predict world population growth over the next 50 or 100 years. We can do that by developing a model that describes how populations grow, fitting the model to the data we have so far, and then using the model to generate predictions. In the next few sections I demonstrate this process, starting with simple models and gradually improving them.

Although there is some curvature in the plotted estimates, it looks like world population growth has been close to linear since 1960 or so. So we'll start with a model that has constant growth. To fit the model to the data, we'll compute the average annual growth from 1950 to 2016. Since the UN and Census data are so close, we'll use the Census data.

We can select a value from a Series using the bracket operator:

```
census[1950]
```

```
2.557628654
```

So we can get the total growth during the interval like this:

```
total_growth = census[2016] - census[1950]
```

In this example, the labels 2016 and 1950 are part of the data, so it would be better not to make them part of the program. Putting values like these in the program is called *hardcoding*; it is considered bad practice because if the data change in the future, we have to change the program.

It would be better to get the labels from the Series. We can do that by selecting the index from census and then selecting the first element:

```
t_0 = census.index[0]
t_0
```

```
1950
```

So t_0 is the label of the first element, which is 1950. We can get the label of the last element like this:

```
t_end = census.index[-1]
t_end
```

```
2016
```

The value -1 indicates the last element; -2 indicates the second-to-last element, and so on.

The difference between t_0 and t_end is the elapsed time between them:

```
elapsed_time = t_end - t_0
elapsed_time
```

```
66
```

Now we can use t_0 and t_end to select the population at the beginning and end of the interval:

```
p_0 = census[t_0]
p_end = census[t_end]
```

and compute the total growth during the interval:

```
total_growth = p_end - p_0
total_growth
```

```
4.768368055
```

Finally, we can compute average annual growth:

```
annual_growth = total_growth / elapsed_time
annual_growth
```

```
0.07224800083333333
```

From 1950 to 2016, world population grew by about 0.07 billion people per year, on average. The next step is to use this estimate to simulate population growth.

Simulating Population Growth

Our simulation will start with the observed population in 1950, p_0, and add annual_growth each year. To store the results, we'll use a TimeSeries object:

```
results = TimeSeries()
```

We can set the first value in the new TimeSeries like this:

```
results[t_0] = p_0
```

Here's what it looks like so far:

```
show(results)
```

Time	Quantity
1950	2.557629

Now we set the rest of the values by simulating annual growth:

```
for t in range(t_0, t_end):
    results[t+1] = results[t] + annual_growth
```

The values of t go from t_0 to t_end, including the first but not the last.

Inside the loop, we compute the population for the next year by adding the population for the current year and annual_growth. The last time through the loop, the value of t is 2015, so the last label in results is 2016.

Here's what the results look like, compared to the estimates:

```
results.plot(color='gray', label='model')
plot_estimates()
decorate(title='Constant growth model')
```

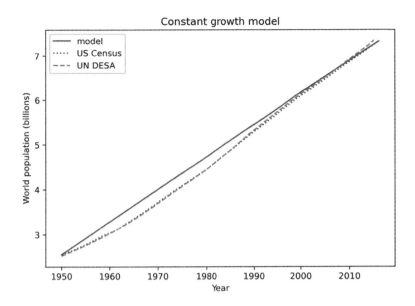

Constant growth model

From 1950 to 1990, the model does not fit the data particularly well, but after that, it's pretty good.

Summary

This chapter was a first step toward modeling changes in world population growth during the last 70 years. We used pandas to read data from a web page and store the results in a DataFrame. From the DataFrame we selected two Series objects and used them to compute absolute and relative errors. Then we computed average population growth and used it to build a simple model with constant annual growth. The model fits recent data pretty well; nevertheless, there are two reasons we should be skeptical:

- There is no obvious mechanism that could cause population growth to be constant from year to year. Changes in population are determined by the fraction of people who die and the fraction of people who give birth, so we expect them to depend on the current population.

- According to this model, world population would keep growing at the same rate forever, and that does not seem reasonable.

In the next chapter we'll consider other models that might fit the data better and make more credible predictions.

Exercise

5.1

Try fitting the model using data from 1970 to the present, and see if that does a better job. Here are some suggestions:

1. Define t_1 to be 1970 and p_1 to be the population in 1970. Use t_1 and p_1 to compute annual growth, but use t_0 and p_0 to run the simulation.

2. You might want to add a constant to the starting value to match the data better.

6

ITERATING THE POPULATION MODEL

 In the previous chapter we simulated a model of world population with constant growth. In this chapter we'll see if we can make a better model with growth proportional to the population. But first, we'll improve the code from the previous chapter by encapsulating it in a function and adding a new feature, a System object.

This chapter is available as a Jupyter notebook where you can read the text, run the code, and work on the exercise. You can access the notebooks at *https://allendowney.github.io/ModSimPy*.

System Objects

Like a State object, a System object contains variables and their values. The difference is:

- State objects contain state variables that get updated in the course of a simulation.

- System objects contain *system parameters*, which usually don't get updated over the course of a simulation.

For example, in the bike share model, state variables include the number of bikes at each location, which get updated whenever a customer moves a bike. System parameters include the number of locations, total number of bikes, and arrival rates at each location.

In the population model, the only state variable is the population. System parameters include the annual growth rate, the initial population, and the start and end times.

Suppose we have the following variables, as computed in the previous chapter (assuming `table2` is the `DataFrame` we read from the file):

```
un = table2.un / 1e9
census = table2.census / 1e9

t_0 = census.index[0]
t_end = census.index[-1]
elapsed_time = t_end - t_0

p_0 = census[t_0]
p_end = census[t_end]

total_growth = p_end - p_0
annual_growth = total_growth / elapsed_time
```

Some of these are parameters we need to simulate the system; others are temporary values we can discard. To distinguish between them, we'll put the parameters we need in a `System` object like this:

```
system = System(t_0=t_0,
                t_end=t_end,
                p_0=p_0,
                annual_growth=annual_growth)
```

Here, t0 and t_end are the first and last years, p_0 is the initial population, and annual_growth is the estimated annual growth.

The assignment t_0=t_0 reads the value of the existing variable named t_0, which we created previously, and stores it in a new system variable, also named t_0. The variables inside the `System` object are distinct from other variables, so you can change one without affecting the other, even if they have the same name. This `System` object contains four new variables:

```
show(system)
```
----

	value
t_0	1950.000000
t_end	2016.000000
p_0	2.557629
annual_growth	0.072248

Next we'll wrap the code from the previous chapter in a function:

```
def run_simulation1(system):
    results = TimeSeries()
    results[system.t_0] = system.p_0

    for t in range(system.t_0, system.t_end):
        results[t+1] = results[t] + system.annual_growth

    return results
```

run_simulation1 takes a System object and reads from it the values of t_0, t_end, and annual_growth. It simulates population growth over time and returns the results in a TimeSeries. Here's how we call it:

```
results1 = run_simulation1(system)
```

Here's the function we used in the previous chapter to plot the estimates:

```
def plot_estimates():
    census.plot(style=':', label='US Census')
    un.plot(style='--', label='UN DESA')
    decorate(xlabel='Year',
             ylabel='World population (billion)')
```

And here are the results:

```
results1.plot(label='model', color='gray')
plot_estimates()
decorate(title='Constant growth model')
```

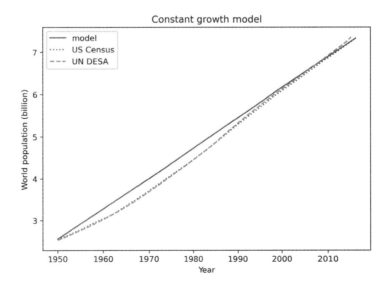

It might not be obvious that using functions and System objects is a big improvement, and for a simple model that we run only once, maybe it's not. But as we work with more complex models, and when we run many simulations with different parameters, we'll see that this way of organizing the code makes a big difference.

Now let's see if we can improve the model.

A Proportional Growth Model

The biggest problem with the constant growth model is that it doesn't make any sense. It is hard to imagine how people all over the world could conspire to keep population growth constant from year to year. If some fraction of the population dies each year, and some fraction gives birth, we can compute the net change in the population like this:

```
def run_simulation2(system):
    results = TimeSeries()
    results[system.t_0] = system.p_0

    for t in range(system.t_0, system.t_end):
        births = system.birth_rate * results[t]
        deaths = system.death_rate * results[t]
        results[t+1] = results[t] + births - deaths

    return results
```

Each time through the loop, we use the parameter birth_rate to compute the number of births, and death_rate to compute the number of deaths. The rest of the function is the same as run_simulation1.

Now we can choose the values of birth_rate and death_rate that best fit the data. For the death rate, we'll use 7.7 deaths per 1,000 people, which was roughly the global death rate in 2020 (*https://www.indexmundi.com/world/death_rate.html*). I chose the birth rate by hand to fit the population data:

```
system.death_rate = 7.7 / 1000
system.birth_rate = 25 / 1000
```

Running the simulation and plotting the results, we get:

```
results2 = run_simulation2(system)
results2.plot(label='model', color='gray')
plot_estimates()
decorate(title='Proportional growth model')
```

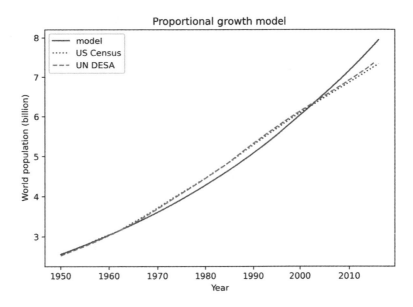

The proportional model fits the data well from 1950 to 1965, but not so well after that. Overall, the *quality of fit* is not as good as the constant growth model, which is surprising, because it seems like the proportional model is more realistic.

In the next chapter we'll try one more time to find a model that makes sense and fits the data. But first, let's make a few more improvements to the code.

Factoring Out the Update Function

run_simulation1 and run_simulation2 are nearly identical except for the body of the for loop, where we compute the population for the next year. Rather than repeat identical code, we can separate the things that change from the things that don't. First, we'll pull out the births and deaths from run_simulation2 and make a function:

```
def growth_func1(t, pop, system):
    births = system.birth_rate * pop
    deaths = system.death_rate * pop
    return births - deaths
```

growth_func1 takes as arguments the current year, current population, and a System object; it returns the net population growth during the current year.

This function does not use t, so we could leave it out. But we will see other growth functions that need it, and it is convenient if they all take the same parameters, used or not. Now we can write a function that runs any model:

```
def run_simulation(system, growth_func):
    results = TimeSeries()
    results[system.t_0] = system.p_0

    for t in range(system.t_0, system.t_end):
        growth = growth_func(t, results[t], system)
        results[t+1] = results[t] + growth

    return results
```

This function demonstrates a feature we have not seen before: it takes a function as a parameter! When we call run_simulation, the second parameter is a function, like growth_func1, that computes the population for the next year.

Here's how we call it:

```
results = run_simulation(system, growth_func1)
```

Passing a function as an argument is the same as passing any other value. The argument, which is growth_func1 in this example, gets assigned to the parameter, which is called growth_func. Inside run_simulation, we can call growth_func just like any other function.

Each time through the loop, run_simulation calls growth_func1 to compute net growth, and uses it to compute the population during the next year.

Combining Birth and Death

We can simplify the code slightly by combining births and deaths to compute the net growth rate. Instead of two parameters, birth_rate and death_rate, we can write the update function in terms of a single parameter that represents the difference:

```
system.alpha = system.birth_rate - system.death_rate
```

The name of this parameter, alpha, is the conventional name for a proportional growth rate.

Here's the modified version of growth_func1:

```
def growth_func2(t, pop, system):
    return system.alpha * pop
```

and here's how we run it:

```
results = run_simulation(system, growth_func2)
```

The results are the same as the previous versions, but now the code is organized in a way that makes it easy to explore other models.

Summary

In this chapter, we wrapped the code from the previous chapter in functions and used a System object to store the parameters of the system.

We explored a new model of population growth, where the number of births and deaths is proportional to the current population. This model seems more realistic, but it turns out not to fit the data particularly well.

In the next chapter, we'll try one more model, which is based on the assumption that the population can't keep growing forever.

Exercise

6.1

Maybe the reason the proportional model doesn't work very well is that the growth rate, alpha, is changing over time. So let's try a model with different growth rates before and after 1980 (as an arbitrary choice).

Write an update function that takes t, pop, and system as parameters. The System object, system, should contain two parameters: the growth rate before 1980, alpha1, and the growth rate after 1980, alpha2. It should use t to determine which growth rate to use.

Test your function by calling it directly, then pass it to run_simulation. Plot the results. Adjust the parameters alpha1 and alpha2 to fit the data as well as you can.

Under the Hood

The System object defined in the ModSim library is based on the SimpleNamespace object defined in a standard Python library called types; the documentation is at *https://docs.python.org/3.7/library/types.html#types.SimpleNamespace*.

7

LIMITS TO GROWTH

In the previous chapter we developed a population model where net growth during each time step is proportional to the current population. This model seems more realistic than the constant growth model, but it does not fit the data as well.

There are a few things we could try to improve the model:

- Maybe net growth depends on the current population, but the relationship is quadratic, not linear.

- Maybe the net growth rate varies over time.

In this chapter, we'll explore the first option. In the exercises, you will have a chance to try the second.

This chapter is available as a Jupyter notebook where you can read the text, run the code, and work on the exercises. You can access the notebooks at *https://allendowney.github.io/ModSimPy*.

Quadratic Growth

It makes sense that net growth should depend on the current population, but maybe it's not a linear relationship, like this:

```
net_growth = system.alpha * pop
```

Maybe it's a quadratic relationship, like this:

```
net_growth = system.alpha * pop + system.beta * pop**2
```

We can test that conjecture with a new update function:

```
def growth_func_quad(t, pop, system):
    return system.alpha * pop + system.beta * pop**2
```

Here's the System object we'll use, initialized with t_0, p_0, and t_end:

```
t_0 = census.index[0]
p_0 = census[t_0]
t_end = census.index[-1]

system = System(t_0=t_0,
                p_0=p_0,
                t_end=t_end)
```

Now we have to add the parameters alpha and beta:

```
system.alpha = 25 / 1000
system.beta = -1.8 / 1000
```

I chose these values by trial and error; we'll see better ways to do it later.
Here's how we run it:

```
results = run_simulation(system, growth_func_quad)
```

And finally, here are the results:

```
results.plot(color='gray', label='model')
plot_estimates()
decorate(title='Quadratic growth model')
```

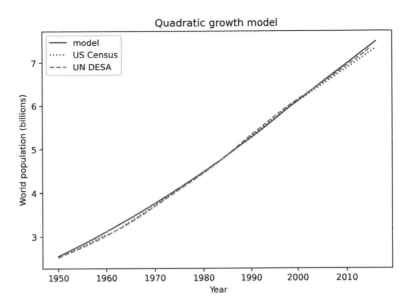

The model fits the data well over the whole range, with just a bit of space between them in the 1960s.

It is not entirely surprising that the quadratic model fits better than the constant and proportional models: it has two parameters we can choose, where the other models have only one. In general, the more parameters you have to play with, the better you should expect the model to fit.

But fitting the data is not the only reason to think the quadratic model might be a good choice. It also makes sense; that is, there is a legitimate reason to expect the relationship between growth and population to have this form. To understand it, let's look at net growth as a function of population.

Net Growth

Let's plot the relationship between growth and population in the quadratic model. We'll use linspace to make an array of 101 populations from 0 to 15 billion:

```
from numpy import linspace

pop_array = linspace(0, 15, 101)
```

Now we'll use the quadratic model to compute net growth for each population:

```
growth_array = (system.alpha * pop_array +
                system.beta * pop_array**2)
```

To plot growth rate versus population, we'll use the `plot` function from Matplotlib. First we have to import it:

```
from matplotlib.pyplot import plot
```

Now we can use it like this:

```
plot(pop_array, growth_array, label='net growth', color='C2')

decorate(xlabel='Population (billions)',
         ylabel='Net growth (billions)',
         title='Net growth vs. population')
```

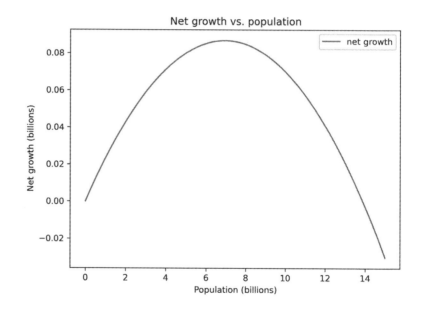

Note that the x-axis is not time, as in the previous figures, but population. We can divide this curve into four kinds of behavior:

- When the population is less than 3 billion, net growth is proportional to population, as in the proportional model. In this range, the population grows slowly because the population is small.

- Between 3 billion and 10 billion, the population grows quickly because there are a lot of people.

- Above 10 billion, population grows more slowly; this behavior models the effect of resource limitations that decrease birth rates or increase death rates.

- Above 14 billion, resources are so limited that the death rate exceeds the birth rate and net growth becomes negative.

Just below 14 billion, there is a point where net growth is 0, which means that the population does not change. At this point, the birth and death rates are equal, so the population is in *equilibrium*.

Finding Equilibrium

The equilibrium point is the population, p, where net population growth, Δp, is 0. We can compute it by finding the roots, or zeros, of this equation:

$$\Delta p = \alpha p + \beta p^2$$

where α and β are the parameters of the model. If we rewrite the right-hand side like this:

$$\Delta p = p(\alpha + \beta p)$$

we can see that net growth is 0 when $p = 0$ or $p = -\alpha/\beta$. So we can compute the (nonzero) equilibrium point like this:

```
-system.alpha / system.beta
```
```
13.88888888888889
```

With these parameters, net growth is 0 when the population is about 13.9 billion (the result is positive because beta is negative).

In the context of population modeling, the quadratic model is more conventionally written like this:

$$\Delta p = rp(1 - p/K)$$

This is the same model; it's just a different way to *parameterize* it. Given α and β, we can compute $r = \alpha$ and $K = -\alpha/\beta$.

In this version, it is easier to interpret the parameters: r is the unconstrained growth rate, observed when p is small, and K is the equilibrium point. K is also called the *carrying capacity*, since it indicates the maximum population the environment can sustain.

Dysfunctions

When people learn about functions, there are a few things they often find confusing. In this section I'll present and explain some common problems.

As an example, suppose you want a function that takes a System object, with variables alpha and beta, and computes the carrying capacity, -alpha/beta.

Here's a good solution:

```
def carrying_capacity(system):
    K = -system.alpha / system.beta
    return K


sys1 = System(alpha=0.025, beta=-0.0018)
pop = carrying_capacity(sys1)
print(pop)
```

```
13.88888888888889
```

Now let's see all the ways this can go wrong.

Dysfunction #1: Not Using Parameters

In the following version, the function doesn't take any parameters; when sys1 appears inside the function, it refers to the object we create outside the function:

```
# WRONG
def carrying_capacity():
    K = -sys1.alpha / sys1.beta
    return K


sys1 = System(alpha=0.025, beta=-0.0018)
pop = carrying_capacity()
print(pop)
```

```
13.88888888888889
```

This version works, but it is not as versatile as it could be. If there are several System objects, this function can work with only one of them, and only if it is named sys1.

Dysfunction #2: Clobbering the Parameters

When people first learn about parameters, they often write functions like this:

```
# WRONG
def carrying_capacity(system):
    system = System(alpha=0.025, beta=-0.0018)
    K = -system.alpha / system.beta
    return K


sys1 = System(alpha=0.03, beta=-0.002)
pop = carrying_capacity(sys1)
print(pop)
```

```
13.88888888888889
```

In this example, we have a `System` object named `sys1` that gets passed as an argument to `carrying_capacity`. But when the function runs, it ignores the argument and immediately replaces it with a new `System` object. As a result, this function always returns the same value, no matter what argument is passed.

When you write a function, you generally don't know what the values of the parameters will be. Your job is to write a function that works for any valid values. If you assign your own values to the parameters, you defeat the whole purpose of functions.

Dysfunction #3: No Return Value

Here's a version that computes the value of `K` but doesn't return it:

```
# WRONG
def carrying_capacity(system):
    K = -system.alpha / system.beta

sys1 = System(alpha=0.025, beta=-0.0018)
pop = carrying_capacity(sys1)
print(pop)
```
```
None
```

A function that doesn't have a return statement actually returns a special value called `None`, so in this example the value of `pop` is `None`. If you are debugging a program and find that the value of a variable is `None` when it shouldn't be, a function without a return statement is a likely cause.

Dysfunction #4: Ignoring the Return Value

Finally, here's a version where the function is correct, but the way it's used is not:

```
def carrying_capacity(system):
    K = -system.alpha / system.beta
    return K

sys1 = System(alpha=0.025, beta=-0.0018)
carrying_capacity(sys1) # WRONG
print(K)
```

In this example, `carrying_capacity` runs and returns `K`, but the return value doesn't get displayed or assigned to a variable. If we try to print `K`, we get a `NameError`, because `K` only exists inside the function.

When you call a function that returns a value, you should do something with the result.

Summary

In this chapter, we implemented a quadratic growth model where net growth depends on the current population and the population squared. This model fits the data well, and we saw one reason why: it is based on the assumption that there is a limit to the number of people the Earth can support.

In the next chapter we'll use the models we have developed to generate predictions.

Exercises

7.1

In this chapter, we saw a different way to parameterize the quadratic model:

$$\Delta p = rp(1 - p/K)$$

where $r = \alpha$ and $K = -\alpha/\beta$.

Write a version of growth_func that implements this version of the model. Test it by computing the values of r and K that correspond to alpha=0.025 and beta=-0.0018, and confirm that you get the same results.

7.2

What happens if we start with an initial population above the carrying capacity, like 20 billion? Run the model with initial populations between 1 and 20 billion, and plot the results on the same axes.

Hint: If there are too many labels in the legend, you can plot results like this:

```
results.plot(label='_nolegend')
```

8

PROJECTING INTO THE FUTURE

In the previous chapter, we developed a quadratic model of world population growth from 1950 to 2016. It is a simple model, but it fits the data well and the mechanisms it's based on are plausible. In this chapter, we will use the quadratic model to generate projections of future growth and compare our results to projections from actual demographers.

This chapter is available as a Jupyter notebook where you can read the text, run the code, and work on the exercise. You can access the notebooks at *https://allendowney.github.io/ModSimPy*.

Generating Projections

Let's run the quadratic model, extending the results until 2100, and see how our projections compare to the professionals'.

Here's the quadratic growth function again:

```
def growth_func_quad(t, pop, system):
    return system.alpha * pop + system.beta * pop**2
```

And here are the system parameters:

```
t_0 = census.index[0]
p_0 = census[t_0]

system = System(t_0=t_0,
                p_0=p_0,
                alpha=25/1000,
                beta=-1.8/1000,
                t_end=2100)
```

With t_end=2100, we can generate the projection by calling run_simulation the usual way:

```
results = run_simulation(system, growth_func_quad)
```

Here are the last few values in the results:

```
show(results.tail())
```

Time	Quantity
2096	12.462519
2097	12.494516
2098	12.525875
2099	12.556607
2100	12.586719

And here's what the results look like:

```
results.plot(color='gray', label='model')
decorate(xlabel='Year',
         ylabel='World population (billions)',
         title='Quadratic model projection')
```

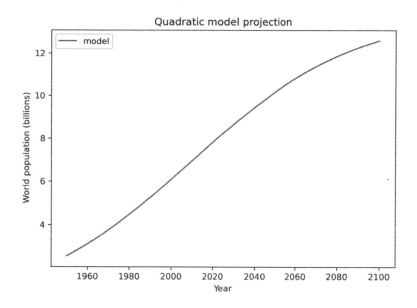

Quadratic model projection

According to the model, population growth will slow gradually after 2020, approaching 12.6 billion by 2100.

I am using the word *projection* deliberately, rather than *prediction*, with the following distinction: *prediction* implies something like "this is what we expect to happen, at least approximately," while *projection* implies something like "if this model is a good description of the system, and if nothing in the future causes the system parameters to change, this is what would happen."

Using *projection* leaves open the possibility that there are important things in the real world that are not captured in the model. It also suggests that, even if the model is good, the parameters we estimate based on the past might be different in the future.

The quadratic model we've been working with is based on the assumption that population growth is limited by the availability of resources; in that scenario, as the population approaches carrying capacity, birth rates fall and death rates rise because resources become scarce. If that assumption is valid, we might be able to use actual population growth to estimate carrying capacity, provided we observe the transition into the population range where the growth rate starts to fall.

But in the case of world population growth, those conditions don't apply. Over the last 50 years, the net growth rate has leveled off, but not yet started to fall, so we don't have enough data to make a credible estimate of carrying capacity. And resource limitations are probably *not* the primary reason growth has slowed. As evidence, consider:

1. The death rate is not increasing; rather, it has declined from 1.9 percent in 1950 to 0.8 percent now. So the decrease in net growth is due entirely to the declining birth rate.

2. The relationship between resources and birth rate is the opposite of what the model assumes; as nations develop and people become more wealthy, birth rates tend to fall.

We should not take too seriously the idea that this model can estimate carrying capacity. But the predictions of a model can be credible even if the assumptions of the model are not strictly true. For example, population growth might behave *as if* it is resource limited, even if the actual mechanism is something else.

In fact, demographers who study population growth often use models similar to ours. In the next section, we'll compare our projections to theirs.

Comparing Projections

From the same Wikipedia page where we got the past population estimates, we'll read table3, which contains projections for population growth over the next 50–100 years, generated by the US Census, UN DESA, and the Population Reference Bureau:

```
table3 = tables[3]
```

The column names are long strings; for convenience, let's replace them with abbreviations:

```
table3.columns = ['census', 'prb', 'un']
```

Here are the first few rows:

```
table3.head()
```

Year	census	prb	un
2016	7.334772e+09	NaN	7.432663e+09
2017	7.412779e+09	NaN	NaN
2018	7.490428e+09	NaN	NaN
2019	7.567403e+09	NaN	NaN
2020	7.643402e+09	NaN	7.758157e+09

Some values are NaN, which indicates missing data, because some organizations did not publish projections for some years. The following function plots projections from the UN DESA and US Census. It uses dropna to remove the NaN values from each series before plotting it:

```
def plot_projections(table):
    """Plot world population projections.

    table: DataFrame with columns 'un' and 'census'
    """
    census_proj = table.census.dropna() / 1e9
    un_proj = table.un.dropna() / 1e9

    census_proj.plot(style=':', label='US Census')
    un_proj.plot(style='--', label='UN DESA')

    decorate(xlabel='Year',
             ylabel='World population (billions)')
```

Here are the professional projections compared to the results of the quadratic model:

```
results.plot(color='gray', label='model')
plot_projections(table3)
decorate(title='Quadratic model projection, with UN and Census')
```

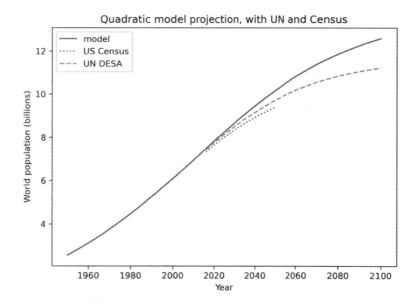

The UN DESA expects the world population to reach 11 billion around 2100 and then level off. Projections by the US Census are a little lower, and they only go until 2050.

Summary

In this chapter, we used the quadratic growth model to project world population growth between now and 2100.

Real demographers expect world population to grow more slowly than our model, probably because their models are broken down by region and country, where conditions are different, and they take into account expected economic development.

Nevertheless, their projections are qualitatively similar to ours, and theirs differ from each other almost as much as they differ from ours. So the results from the model, simple as it is, are not entirely unreasonable.

If you are interested in some of the factors that go into the professional projections, you might like this video by Hans Rosling about the demographic changes we expect this century: *https://www.youtube.com/watch?v=ezVk1ahRF78*.

Exercise

8.1

The net growth rate of world population has been declining for several decades. That observation suggests one more way to generate more realistic projections: by extrapolating observed changes in growth rate.

To compute past growth rates, we'll use a function called diff, which computes the difference between successive elements in a Series. For example, here are the changes from one year to the next in census:

```
diff = census.diff()
show(diff.head())
```

Year	census
1950	NaN
1951	0.037311
1952	0.041832
1953	0.045281
1954	0.048175

The first element is NaN because we don't have the data for 1949, so we can't compute the first difference.

If we divide these differences by the populations, the result is an estimate of the growth rate during each year:

```
alpha = census.diff() / census
show(alpha.head())
```

Year	census
1950	NaN
1951	0.014378
1952	0.015865
1953	0.016883
1954	0.017645

The following function computes and plots the growth rates for the census and un estimates:

```
def plot_alpha():
    alpha_census = census.diff() / census
    alpha_census.plot(style='.', label='US Census')

    alpha_un = un.diff() / un
    alpha_un.plot(style='.', label='UN DESA')

    decorate(xlabel='Year', ylabel='Net growth rate')
```

It uses style='.' to plot each data point with a small circle. And here's what it looks like:

```
plot_alpha()
```

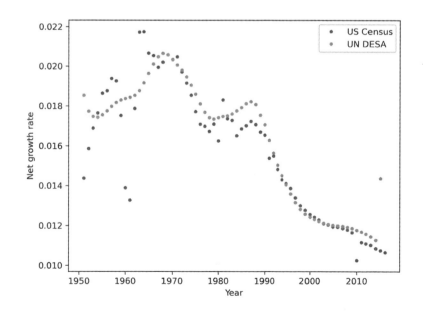

Other than a bump around 1990, the net growth rate has been declining roughly linearly since 1970.

We can model the decline by fitting a line to this data and extrapolating into the future. Here's a function that takes a timestamp and
computes a line that roughly fits the growth rates since 1970:

```
def alpha_func(t):
    intercept = 0.02
    slope = -0.00021
    return intercept + slope * (t - 1970)
```

To see what it looks like, let's create an array of timestamps from
1960 to 2020 and use alpha_func to compute the corresponding growth
rates:

```
t_array = linspace(1960, 2020, 5)
alpha_array = alpha_func(t_array)
```

Here's what it looks like, compared to the data:

```
from matplotlib.pyplot import plot

plot_alpha()
plot(t_array, alpha_array, label='model', color='gray')

decorate(ylabel='Net growth rate',
         title='Linear model of net growth rate')
```

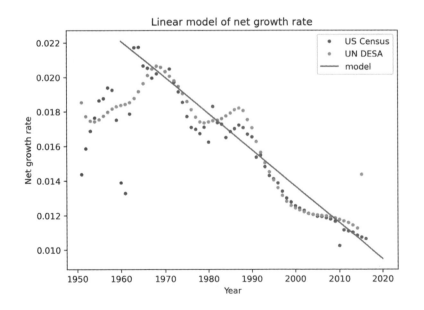

If you don't like the slope and intercept I chose, feel free to adjust them.

Now, as an exercise, you can use this function to project world population until 2100.

1. Create a System object that includes alpha_func as a parameter.
2. Define a growth function that uses alpha_func to compute the net growth rate at the given time t.
3. Run a simulation from 1960 to 2100 with your growth function, and plot the results.
4. Compare your projections with those from the US Census and UN DESA.

9

ANALYSIS AND SYMBOLIC COMPUTATION

 In this chapter we'll express the models from previous chapters as difference equations and differential equations, solve the equations, and derive the functional forms of the solutions. I'll also present some thoughts about the complementary roles of mathematical analysis and simulation.

This chapter is available as a Jupyter notebook where you can read the text, run the code, and work on the exercises. You can access the notebooks at *https://allendowney.github.io/ModSimPy*.

Difference Equations

The population models in the previous chapter and this one are simple enough that we didn't really need to run simulations. We could have solved them mathematically. For example, we wrote the constant growth model like this:

```
results[t+1] = results[t] + annual_growth
```

In mathematical notation, we would write the same model like this:

$$x_{n+1} = x_n + c$$

where x_n is the population during year n, x_{n+1} is the population during year $n+1$, and c is constant annual growth. This way of representing the model, where future population is a function of current population, is a *difference equation*.

For a given value of n, sometimes it is possible to compute x_n directly—that is, without computing the intervening values from x_1 through x_{n-1}. In the case of constant growth, we can see that $x_1 = x_0 + c$, and $x_2 = x_1 + c$. Combining these, we get $x_2 = x_0 + 2c$, then $x_3 = x_0 + 3c$, and we can see that, in general:

$$x_n = x_0 + nc$$

So if we want to know x_{100} and we don't care about the other values, we can compute it with one multiplication and one addition.

We can also write the proportional model as a difference equation:

$$x_{n+1} = x_n + \alpha x_n$$

or more conventionally as:

$$x_{n+1} = x_n(1 + \alpha)$$

Now we can see that $x_1 = x_0(1 + \alpha)$, and $x_2 = x_0(1 + \alpha)^2$, and in general:

$$x_n = x_0(1 + \alpha)^n$$

A sequence with this functional form is called a *geometric progression*. When α is positive, the factor $1 + \alpha$ is greater than 1, so the elements of the sequence grow without bound.

Finally, we can write the quadratic model like this:

$$x_{n+1} = x_n + \alpha x_n + \beta x_n^2$$

or with the more conventional parameterization like this:

$$x_{n+1} = x_n + r x_n(1 - x_n/K)$$

There is no analytic solution to this equation, but we can approximate it with a differential equation and solve that, which is what we'll do in the next section.

Differential Equations

Starting again with the constant growth model

$$x_{n+1} = x_n + c$$

if we define Δx to be the change in x from one time step to the next, we can write:

$$\Delta x = x_{n+1} - x_n = c$$

If we define Δt to be the time step, which is one year in the example, we can write the rate of change per unit of time like this:

$$\frac{\Delta x}{\Delta t} = c$$

This is a *discrete* model, which means time is only defined at integer values of n and not in between. But in reality, people are born and die all the time, not once a year, so it might be more realistic to use a *continuous* model, which means time is defined at all values of t, not just integers.

In a continuous model, we write the rate of change in the form of a derivative:

$$\frac{dx}{dt} = c$$

This way of representing the model is a *differential equation*, which is an equation that involves at least one derivative.

To solve this equation, we multiply both sides by dt:

$$dx = c\,dt$$

and then integrate both sides:

$$x(t) = ct + x_0$$

Similarly, we can write the proportional growth model like this:

$$\frac{\Delta x}{\Delta t} = \alpha x$$

and as a differential equation like this:

$$\frac{dx}{dt} = \alpha x$$

If we multiply both sides by dt and divide by x, we get:

$$\frac{1}{x}\,dx = \alpha\,dt$$

Now we integrate both sides, yielding:

$$\ln x = \alpha t + K$$

where ln is the natural logarithm and K is the constant of integration.

Exponentiating both sides, we have:

$$\exp(\ln(x)) = \exp(\alpha t + K)$$

The exponential function can be written $\exp(x)$ or e^x. In this book I use the first form because it resembles the Python code.

We can rewrite the previous equation as:

$$x = \exp(\alpha t)\exp(K)$$

Since K is an arbitrary constant, $\exp(K)$ is also an arbitrary constant, so we can write:

$$x = C\exp(\alpha t)$$

where $C = \exp(K)$. There are many solutions to this differential equation, with different values of C. The particular solution we want is the one that has the value x_0 when $t = 0$.

When $t = 0$, $x(t) = C$, so $C = x_0$, and the solution we want is:

$$x(t) = x_0\exp(\alpha t)$$

If you would like to see this derivation done more carefully, you might like this video: *https://www.khanacademy.org/math/old-ap-calculus-ab/ab -diff-equations/ab-exp-models/v/exponential-solution-to-differential-equation*.

Analysis and Simulation

Once you have designed a model, there are generally two ways to proceed: simulation and analysis. Simulation often comes in the form of a computer program that models changes in a system over time, like births and deaths, or bikes moving from place to place. Analysis often comes in the form of algebra and calculus—that is, symbolic manipulation using mathematical notation.

Analysis and simulation have different capabilities and limitations. Simulation is generally more versatile; it is easy to add and remove parts of a program and test many versions of a model, as we have done in the previous examples.

But there are several things we can do with analysis that are harder or impossible with simulations:

- With analysis we can sometimes compute, exactly and efficiently, a value that we could only approximate, less efficiently, with simulation. For example, in the quadratic model we plotted net growth versus population and saw that it crosses through zero when the population is near 14 billion. We could estimate the crossing point using a numerical search algorithm (more about that later). But with a bit of algebra, we derived the general result that $K = -\alpha/\beta$.

- Analysis sometimes provides "computational shortcuts," that is, the ability to jump forward in time to compute the state of a system many time steps in the future without computing the intervening states.

- We can use analysis to state and prove generalizations about models; for example, we might prove that certain results will always or never occur. With simulations, we can show examples and sometimes find counterexamples, but it is hard to write proofs.

- Analysis can provide insight into models and the systems they describe; for example, sometimes we can identify qualitatively different ways the system can behave and key parameters that control those behaviors.

When people see what analysis can do, they sometimes get drunk with power and imagine that it gives them a special ability to see past the veil of the material world and discern the laws of mathematics that govern the universe. When they analyze a model of a physical system, they talk about "the math behind it" as if our world is the mere shadow of a world of ideal mathematical entities (I am not making this up; see *https://en.wikipedia.org/wiki/Allegory_of_the_cave*).

This is, of course, nonsense. Mathematical notation is a language designed by humans for a purpose, specifically to facilitate symbolic manipulations like algebra. Similarly, programming languages are designed for a purpose, specifically to represent computational ideas and run programs.

Each of these languages is good for the purposes it was designed for and less good for other purposes. But they are often complementary, and one of the goals of this book is to show how they can be used together.

Analysis with WolframAlpha

Until recently, most analysis was done by rubbing graphite on wood pulp, a process that is laborious and error-prone. A useful alternative is symbolic computation. If you have used services like WolframAlpha, you have used symbolic computation.

For example, if you go to *https://www.wolframalpha.com* and enter

```
df(t) / dt = alpha f(t)
```

WolframAlpha infers that f(t) is a function of t and alpha is a parameter; it classifies the query as a "first-order linear ordinary differential equation" and reports the general solution:

$$f(t) = c_1 \exp(\alpha t)$$

If you add a second equation to specify the initial condition

```
df(t) / dt = alpha f(t), f(0) = p_0
```

WolframAlpha reports the particular solution:

$$f(t) = p_0 \exp(\alpha t)$$

WolframAlpha is based on Mathematica, a powerful programming language designed specifically for symbolic computation.

Analysis with SymPy

Python has a library called SymPy that provides symbolic computation tools similar to Mathematica. They are not as easy to use as WolframAlpha, but they have some other advantages. To use SymPy, we'll define Symbol objects that represent names of variables and functions. The symbols function takes a string and returns Symbol objects. So if we run this assignment

```
from sympy import symbols

t = symbols('t')
```

and then use t in an expression, Python treats it like a variable name rather than a specific number; for example:

```
expr = t + 1
expr
```
- -
$t + 1$

Python doesn't try to perform numerical addition; rather, it creates a new Symbol that represents the sum of t and 1. We can evaluate the sum using subs, which substitutes a value for a symbol. This example substitutes 2 for t:

```
expr.subs(t, 2)
```
- -
3

Functions in SymPy are represented by a special kind of Symbol:

```
from sympy import Function

f = Function('f')
f
```
- -
f

Now if we write f(t), we get an object that represents the evaluation of a function, f, at a value, t:

```
f(t)
```
- -
$f(t)$

But again, SymPy doesn't actually try to evaluate it.

Differential Equations in SymPy

SymPy provides a function, diff, that can differentiate a function. We can apply it to f(t) like this:

```
from sympy import diff

dfdt = diff(f(t), t)
dfdt
```

$$\frac{d}{dt}f(t)$$

The result is a `Symbol` that represents the derivative of `f` with respect to `t`. But again, SymPy doesn't try to compute the derivative yet. If you run this code in a Jupyter notebook (recommended), the output should be formatted to look like math notation. If you run the code in another Python environment, you might see something that looks more like computer code. The examples here will work either way; the results are just displayed differently.

To represent a differential equation, we use `Eq`:

```
from sympy import Eq

alpha = symbols('alpha')
eq1 = Eq(dfdt, alpha*f(t))
eq1
```

$$\frac{d}{dt}f(t) = \alpha f(t)$$

The result is an object that represents an equation.

Now we can use `dsolve` to solve this differential equation:

```
from sympy import dsolve

solution_eq = dsolve(eq1)
solution_eq
```

$$f(t) = C_1 e^{\alpha t}$$

The result is the *general solution*, which still contains an unspecified constant, C_1. To get the *particular solution* where $f(0) = p_0$, we substitute p_0 for `C1`. First, we have to tell Python that `C1` is a symbol:

```
C1 = symbols('C1')
```

Now we can substitute the value of p_0 for `C1`. For example, if p_0 is 1,000:

```
particular = solution_eq.subs(C1, 1000)
particular
```

$$f(t) = 1000 e^{\alpha t}$$

When $t = 0$, the value of $f(0)$ is p_0:

```
particular.subs(t, 0)
```

$$f(0) = 1000$$

That confirms that this is the solution we want.

Solving the Quadratic Growth Model

To solve the quadratic growth equation, we'll use the `r, K` parameterization, so we'll need two more symbols:

```
r, K = symbols('r K')
```

Now we can write the differential equation:

```
eq2 = Eq(diff(f(t), t), r * f(t) * (1 - f(t)/K))
eq2
```

$$\frac{d}{dt}f(t) = r\left(1 - \frac{f(t)}{K}\right)f(t)$$

and solve it:

```
solution_eq = dsolve(eq2)
solution_eq
```

$$f(t) = \frac{Ke^{C_1 K + rt}}{e^{C_1 K + rt} - 1}$$

The result, `solution_eq`, contains `rhs`, which is the right-hand side of the solution:

```
general = solution_eq.rhs
general
```

$$\frac{Ke^{C_1 K + rt}}{e^{C_1 K + rt} - 1}$$

We can evaluate the right-hand side at $t = 0$:

```
at_0 = general.subs(t, 0)
at_0
```

$$\frac{Ke^{C_1 K}}{e^{C_1 K} - 1}$$

Now we want to find the value of `C1` that makes `f(0)` = `p_0`. So we'll create the equation `at_0` = `p_0` and solve for `C1`. Because this is just an algebraic equation, not a differential equation, we use `solve`, not `dsolve`:

```
from sympy import solve

p_0 = symbols('p_0')
solutions = solve(Eq(at_0, p_0), C1)
```

The result from `solve` is a list of solutions:

```
type(solutions), len(solutions)
```

```
(list, 1)
```

In this case, there is only one solution, but we still get a list, so we have to use the bracket operator, `[0]`, to select the first one:

```
value_of_C1 = solutions[0]
value_of_C1
```

$$\frac{\log\left(-\frac{p_0}{K-p_0}\right)}{K}$$

In the general solution, we want to replace `C1` with the value of `C1` we just figured out:

```
particular = general.subs(C1, value_of_C1)
particular
```

$$-\frac{Kp_0\,e^{rt}}{(K-p_0)\left(-\frac{p_0\,e^{rt}}{K-p_0}-1\right)}$$

The result is complicated, but SymPy provides a function that tries to simplify it:

```
simpler = particular.simplify()
simpler
```

$$\frac{Kp_0\,e^{rt}}{K+p_0\,e^{rt}-p_0}$$

This function is called the *logistic growth curve*; see *http://modsimpy.com/logistic*. In the context of growth models, the logistic function is often written like this:

$$f(t) = \frac{K}{1 + A\exp(-rt)}$$

where $A = (K - p_0)/p_0$.

If you would like to see this differential equation solved by hand, you might like this video: *https://www.khanacademy.org/math/old-ap-calculus-bc/bc-diff-equations/bc-logistic-models/v/solving-logistic-differential-equation-part-1.*

Summary

In this chapter, we wrote the growth models from the previous chapters in terms of difference and differential equations. We solved some of these equations by hand; for others, we used WolframAlpha and SymPy.

What I called the "constant growth" model is more commonly called *linear growth* because the solution is a line. If we model time as continuous, the solution is

$$f(t) = p_0 + ct$$

where c is net annual growth.

Similarly, the proportional growth model is usually called *exponential growth* because the solution is an exponential function:

$$f(t) = p_0 \exp \alpha t$$

Finally, the quadratic growth model is called *logistic growth* because the solution is a logistic function:

$$f(t) = \frac{K}{1 + A \exp(-rt)}$$

where $A = (K - p_0)/p_0$. I avoided these terms until now because they are based on results we had not derived yet.

With that, we are done modeling world population growth. The next chapter presents case studies where you can apply the tools we have learned so far.

Exercises

9.1

Use SymPy to solve the quadratic growth equation using the alternative parameterization:

$$\frac{df(t)}{dt} = \alpha f(t) + \beta f^2(t)$$

9.2

Use *https://www.wolframalpha.com* to solve the quadratic growth model, using either or both forms of parameterization:

```
df(t) / dt = alpha f(t) + beta f(t)^2
```

or

```
df(t) / dt = r f(t) (1 - f(t)/K)
```

Find the general solution and also the particular solution where f(0) = p_0.

10

CASE STUDIES PART I

This chapter presents case studies where you can apply the tools we have learned so far to problems involving population growth, queueing systems, and tree growth.

This chapter is available as a Jupyter notebook where you can read the text, run the code, and work on the case studies. You can access the notebooks at *https://allendowney.github.io/ModSimPy*.

Historical World Population

The Wikipedia page about world population growth includes estimates for world population from 12,000 years ago to the present (*https://en.wikipedia.org/wiki/World_population_estimates.html*). The following figure shows the estimates of several research groups from 1 CE to the near present:

```
table1.plot()
decorate(xlim=[0, 2000], xlabel='Year',
         ylabel='World population (millions)',
         title='CE population estimates')
```

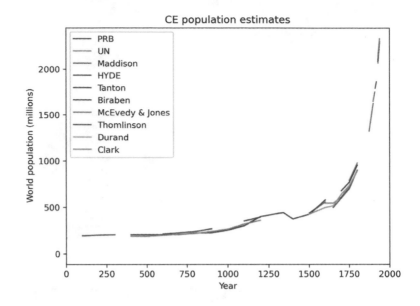

See if you can find a model that fits these estimates. How well does your best model predict actual population growth from 1940 to the present?

One Queue or Two?

This case study is related to *queueing theory*, which is the study of systems that involve waiting in lines, also known as "queues."

Suppose you are designing the checkout area for a new store. There is enough room in the store for two checkout counters and a waiting area for customers. You can make two lines, one for each counter, or one line that feeds both counters.

In theory, you might expect a single line to be better, but it has some practical drawbacks: in order to maintain a single line, you might have to install barriers, and customers might be put off by what seems to be a longer line, even if it moves faster. So you'd like to check whether the single line is really better and by how much. Simulation can help answer this question.

Figure 10-1 shows the three scenarios we'll consider.

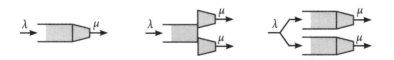

Figure 10-1: One queue, one server (left); one queue, two servers (middle); two queues, two servers (right)

As we did in the bike share model, we'll divide time into discrete time steps of one minute, and we'll assume that a customer is equally likely to arrive during any time step. I'll denote this probability using the Greek letter lambda, λ, or the variable name lam. The value of λ probably varies from day to day, so we'll have to consider a range of possibilities.

Based on data from other stores, you know that it takes five minutes for a customer to check out, on average. But checkout times are variable: most customers take less than five minutes, but some take substantially more. A simple way to model this variability is to assume that when a customer is checking out, they always have the same probability of finishing during the next time step, regardless of how long they have been checking out. I'll denote this probability using the Greek letter mu, μ, or the variable name mu.

If we choose $\mu = 1/5$ per minute, the average time for each checkout will be five minutes, which is consistent with the data.

Now we're ready to implement the model. In the repository for this book, you'll find a notebook called *queue.ipynb* that contains some code to get you started, along with instructions. You can download it from *https://github.com/AllenDowney/ModSimPy/raw/master/examples/queue.ipy* or run it on Colab at *https://colab.research.google.com/github/AllenDowney/ModSimPy/blob/master/examples/queue.ipynb*.

As always, you should practice incremental development: write no more than one or two lines of code at a time, and test as you go!

Predicting Salmon Populations

Each year the US Atlantic Salmon Assessment Committee reports estimates of salmon populations in oceans and rivers in the northeastern United States. The reports are useful for monitoring changes in these populations, but they generally do not include predictions.

The goal of this case study is to model year-to-year changes in population, evaluate how predictable these changes are, and estimate the probability that a particular population will increase or decrease in the next 10 years. As an example, you'll use data from the 2017 report, which provides population estimates for the Narraguagus and Sheepscot Rivers in Maine.

In the repository for this book, you'll find a notebook called *salmon.ipynb* that contains this data and some code to get you started. You can download it from *https://github.com/AllenDowney/ModSimPy/raw/master/examples/salmon.ipynb* or run it on Colab at *https://colab.research.google.com/github/AllenDowney/ModSimPy/blob/master/examples/salmon.ipynb*.

You should take my instructions as suggestions; if you want to try something different, please do!

Tree Growth

This case study is based on "Height-Age Curves for Planted Stands of Douglas Fir, with Adjustments for Density," a working paper by Flewelling et al. It provides *site index curves*, which are curves that show the expected height of the tallest tree in a stand of Douglas fir as a function of age, for a stand where the trees are the same age. Depending on the quality of the site, the trees might grow more quickly or slowly. So each curve is identified by a *site index* that indicates the quality of the site. The goal of this case study is to explain the shape of these curves—that is, why trees grow the way they do. The answer I propose involves fractal dimensions, so you might find it interesting.

In the repository for this book, you'll find a notebook called *trees.ipynb* that incrementally develops a model of tree growth and uses it to fit the data. You can download it from *https://github.com/AllenDowney/ModSimPy/ raw/master/examples/trees.ipynb* or run it on Colab at *https://colab.research .google.com/github/AllenDowney/ModSimPy/blob/master/examples/trees.ipynb*.

There are no exercises in this case study, but it is an example of what you can do with the tools we have so far, and a preview of what you will be able to do with the tools in the next few chapters.

PART II

FIRST-ORDER SYSTEMS

11

EPIDEMIOLOGY AND SIR MODELS

In this chapter, we'll develop a model of an epidemic as it spreads in a susceptible population, and use it to evaluate the effectiveness of possible interventions.

My presentation of the model in the next few chapters is based on an excellent article by David Smith and Lang Moore, "The SIR Model for Spread of Disease," published in the *Journal of Online Mathematics and Its Applications* in December 2001 (*https://www.maa.org/press/periodicals/loci/joma/ the-sir-model-for-spread-of-disease*).

This chapter is available as a Jupyter notebook, where you can read the text, run the code, and work on the exercise. You can access the notebook at *https://allendowney.github.io/ModSimPy/*.

The Freshman Plague

Every year at Olin College, about 90 new students come to campus from around the country and the world. Most of them arrive healthy and happy, but usually at least one brings with them some kind of infectious disease. A few weeks later, predictably, some fraction of the incoming class comes down with what we call the "Freshman Plague."

In this chapter we'll introduce a well-known model of infectious disease, the Kermack-McKendrick (KM) model, and use it to explain the progression of the disease over the course of the semester, to predict the effect of possible interventions (like immunization), and to design the most effective intervention campaign.

So far we have done our own modeling; that is, we've chosen physical systems, identified factors that seem important, and made decisions about how to represent them. In this chapter we start with an existing model and reverse engineer it. Along the way we consider the modeling decisions that went into it and identify its capabilities and limitations.

The Kermack-McKendrick Model

The KM model is an example of an *SIR model*, so named because it represents three categories of people:

S   People who are "susceptible," that is, capable of contracting the disease if they come into contact with someone who is infected.

I   People who are "infectious," that is, capable of passing along the disease if they come into contact with someone who is susceptible.

R   People who have "recovered." In the basic version of the model, people who have recovered are considered to be no longer infectious and immune to reinfection. That is a reasonable model for some diseases, but not for others, so it should be on the list of assumptions to reconsider later.

Let's think about how the number of people in each category changes over time. Suppose we know that people with the disease are infectious for a period of four days, on average. If 100 people are infectious at a particular point in time, and we ignore the particular time each one became infected, we expect about one out of four to recover on any particular day.

Putting that a different way, if the time between infection and recovery is four days, the recovery rate is about 0.25 recoveries per day, which we'll denote with the Greek letter gamma, γ, or the variable name gamma.

If the total number of people in the population is N, and the fraction currently infectious is i, the total number of recoveries we expect per day is $\gamma i N$.

Now let's think about the number of new infections. Suppose we know that each susceptible person comes into contact with one person every three days, on average, in a way that would cause them to become infected if the other person is infected. We'll denote this contact rate with the Greek letter beta, β, or the variable name beta. It's probably not reasonable to assume that we know β ahead of time, but later we'll see how to estimate it based on data from previous outbreaks.

If s is the fraction of the population that's susceptible, sN is the number of susceptible people, βsN is the number of contacts per day, and βsiN is the number of those contacts where the other person is infectious.

In summary:

- The number of recoveries we expect per day is $\gamma i N$; dividing by N yields the fraction of the population that recovers in a day, which is γi.

- The number of new infections we expect per day is $\beta s i N$; dividing by N yields the fraction of the population that gets infected in a day, which is $\beta s i$.

The KM model assumes that the population is closed; that is, no one arrives or departs, so the size of the population, N, is constant.

The KM Equations

If we treat time as a continuous quantity, we can write differential equations that describe the rates of change for s, i, and r (where r is the fraction of the population that has recovered):

$$\frac{ds}{dt} = -\beta s i$$

$$\frac{di}{dt} = \beta s i - \gamma i$$

$$\frac{dr}{dt} = \gamma i$$

To avoid cluttering the equations, I leave it implied that s is a function of time, $s(t)$, and likewise for i and r.

SIR models are examples of *compartment models*, so called because they divide the world into discrete categories, or compartments, and describe transitions from one compartment to another. Compartments are also called *stocks* and transitions between them are called *flows*.

In this example there are three stocks (susceptible, infectious, and recovered) and two flows (new infections and recoveries). Compartment models are often represented visually using stock and flow diagrams. Refer to Figure 11-1, which shows the stock and flow diagram for the KM model.

Figure 11-1: A stock and flow diagram for the KM model

Stocks are represented by rectangles; flows are represented by arrows. The widget in the middle of an arrow represents a valve that controls the rate of flow; Figure 11-1 shows the parameters that control the valves.

Implementing the KM Model

For a given physical system, there are many possible models, and for a given model, there are many ways to represent it. For example, we can represent an SIR model as a stock and flow diagram, as a set of differential equations, or as a Python program. The process of representing a model in these forms is called *implementation*. In this section we'll implement the KM model in Python.

We represent the initial state of the system using a State object with state variables s, i, and r; they represent the fraction of the population in each compartment.

We can initialize the State object with the *number* of people in each compartment; for example, here is the initial state with 1 infected student in a class of 90:

```
init = State(s=89, i=1, r=0)
show(init)
```

	state
s	89
i	1
r	0

We can convert the numbers to fractions by dividing by the total:

```
init /= init.sum()
show(init)
```

	state
s	0.988889
i	0.011111
r	0.000000

For now, let's assume we know the time between contacts and time between infection and recovery:

```
tc = 3 # time between contacts in days
tr = 4 # recovery time in days
```

We can use them to compute the parameters of the model:

```
beta = 1 / tc # contact rate (per day)
gamma = 1 / tr # recovery rate (per day)
```

We'll use a System object to store the parameters and initial conditions. The following function takes the system parameters and returns a new System object:

```
def make_system(beta, gamma):
    init = State(s=89, i=1, r=0)
    init /= init.sum()

    return System(init=init, t_end=7*14,
                  beta=beta, gamma=gamma)
```

The default value for t_end is 14 weeks, about the length of a semester.

Here's what the System object looks like:

```
system = make_system(beta, gamma)
show(system)
```

	value
init	s 0.988889 i 0.011111 r 0.000000 Name...
t_end	98
beta	0.333333
gamma	0.25

Now that we have an object to represent the system and its state, we are ready for the update function.

The Update Function

The purpose of an update function is to take the current state of a system and compute the state during the next time step. Here's the update function we'll use for the KM model:

```
def update_func(t, state, system):
    s, i, r = state.s, state.i, state.r

    infected = system.beta * i * s
    recovered = system.gamma * i

    s -= infected
    i += infected - recovered
    r += recovered

    return State(s=s, i=i, r=r)
```

update_func takes as parameters the current time, a State object, and a System object.

The first line unpacks the State object, assigning the values of the state variables to new variables with the same names. This is an example of *multiple assignment*. The left side is a sequence of variables; the right side is a sequence of expressions. The values on the right side are assigned to the variables on the left side in order. By creating these variables, we avoid repeating state several times, which makes the code easier to read.

The update function computes infected and recovered as a fraction of the population, then updates s, i, and r. The return value is a State that contains the updated values.

We can call update_func like this:

```
state = update_func(0, init, system)
show(state)
```

	state
s	0.985226
i	0.011996
r	0.002778

The result is the new State object.

You might notice that this version of update_func does not use one of its parameters, t. I include it anyway because update functions sometimes depend on time, and it is convenient if they all take the same parameters, whether they need them or not.

Running the Simulation

Now we can simulate the model over a sequence of time steps:

```
def run_simulation1(system, update_func):
    state = system.init

    for t in range(0, system.t_end):
        state = update_func(t, state, system)

    return state
```

The parameters of run_simulation1 are the System object and the update function. The System object contains the parameters, initial conditions, and values of 0 and t_end.

We can call `run_simulation1` like this:

```
final_state = run_simulation1(system, update_func)
show(final_state)
```

	state
s	0.520568
i	0.000666
r	0.478766

The result indicates that after 14 weeks (98 days), about 52 percent of the population is still susceptible, which means they were never infected; almost 48 percent have recovered, which means they were infected at some point; and less than 1 percent are actively infected.

Collecting the Results

The previous version of `run_simulation` returns only the final state, but we might want to see how the state changes over time. We'll consider two ways to do that: first using three `TimeSeries` objects and then using a new object called a `TimeFrame`.

Here's the first version:

```
def run_simulation2(system, update_func):
    S = TimeSeries()
    I = TimeSeries()
    R = TimeSeries()

    state = system.init
    S[0], I[0], R[0] = state

    for t in range(0, system.t_end):
        state = update_func(t, state, system)
        S[t+1], I[t+1], R[t+1] = state.s, state.i, state.r

    return S, I, R
```

First, we create `TimeSeries` objects to store the results. Next, we initialize `state` and the first elements of `S`, `I`, and `R`.

Inside the loop, we use `update_func` to compute the state of the system at the next time step, and then we use multiple assignment to unpack the elements of `state`, assigning each to the corresponding `TimeSeries`.

At the end of the function, we return the values `S`, `I`, and `R`. This is the first example we have seen where a function returns more than one value.

We can run the function like this:

```
S, I, R = run_simulation2(system, update_func)
```

We'll use the following function to plot the results:

```
def plot_results(S, I, R):
    S.plot(style='--', label='Susceptible')
    I.plot(style='-', label='Infected')
    R.plot(style=':', label='Recovered')
    decorate(xlabel='Time (days)',
             ylabel='Fraction of population')
```

We can run it like this:

```
plot_results(S, I, R)
```

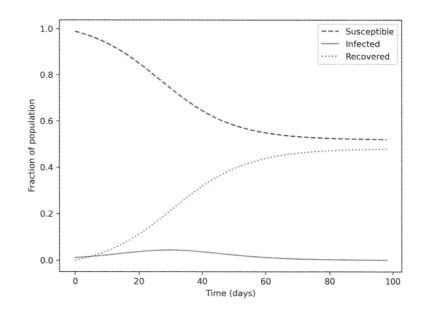

It takes about three weeks (21 days) for the outbreak to get going and about five weeks (35 days) to peak. The fraction of the population that's infected is never very high, but it adds up. In total, almost half the population gets sick.

Now with a TimeFrame

If the number of state variables is small, storing them as separate TimeSeries objects might not be so bad. But a better alternative is to use a TimeFrame, which is another object defined in the ModSim library. A TimeFrame is a kind of DataFrame, which we used earlier to store world population estimates.

Here's a more concise version of run_simulation using a TimeFrame:

```
def run_simulation(system, update_func):
    frame = TimeFrame(columns=system.init.index)
    frame.loc[0] = system.init

    for t in range(0, system.t_end):
        frame.loc[t+1] = update_func(t, frame.loc[t], system)

    return frame
```

The first line creates an empty TimeFrame with one column for each state variable. Then, before the loop starts, we store the initial conditions in the TimeFrame at 0. Based on the way we've been using TimeSeries objects, it is tempting to write

```
frame[0] = system.init
```

but when you use the bracket operator with a TimeFrame or DataFrame, it selects a column, not a row.

To select a row, we have to use loc, like this:

```
frame.loc[0] = system.init
```

Since the value on the right side is a State, the assignment matches up the index of the State with the columns of the TimeFrame; that is, it assigns the s value from system.init to the s column of frame, and likewise with i and r.

During each pass through the loop, we assign the State we get from update_func to the next row of frame. At the end, we return frame.

We can call this version of run_simulation like this:

```
results = run_simulation(system, update_func)
```

Here are the first few rows of the results:

```
results.head()
```

	s	i	r
0	0.988889	0.011111	0.000000
1	0.985226	0.011996	0.002778
2	0.981287	0.012936	0.005777
3	0.977055	0.013934	0.009011
4	0.972517	0.014988	0.012494

The columns in the TimeFrame correspond to the state variables, s, i, and r.

As with a DataFrame, we can use the dot operator to select columns from a TimeFrame, so we can plot the results like this:

```
plot_results(results.s, results.i, results.r)
```

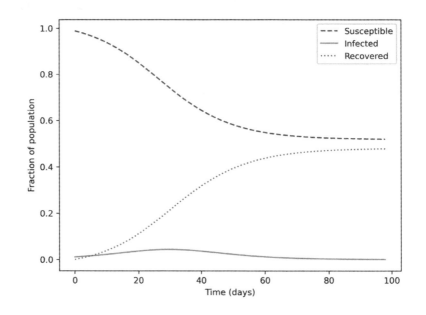

The results are the same as before, now in a more convenient form.

Summary

This chapter presented an SIR model of infectious disease and two ways to collect the results, using several TimeSeries objects or a single TimeFrame. In the next chapter we'll use the model to explore the effect of immunization.

Exercise

11.1

Suppose the time between contacts is four days and the recovery time is five days. After 14 weeks, how many students have been infected in total?

Hint: What is the change in S between the beginning and the end of the simulation?

12

QUANTIFYING INTERVENTIONS

In the previous chapter, I presented the Kermack-McKendrick (KM) model of infectious disease and used it to model the Freshman Plague at Olin. In this chapter, we'll consider metrics intended to quantify the effects of the disease and interventions intended to reduce those effects.

We'll use some of the functions from the previous chapter: make_system, update_func, and the last version of run_simulation, which returns the results in a TimeFrame object.

This chapter is available as a Jupyter notebook where you can read the text, run the code, and work on the exercise. You can access the notebooks at *https://allendowney.github.io/ModSimPy*.

The Effects of Immunization

Models like this are useful for testing "what if" scenarios. As an example, we'll consider the effect of immunization. Suppose there is a vaccine that causes a student to become immune to the Freshman Plague without being infected. How might you modify the model to capture this effect?

One option is to treat immunization as a shortcut from susceptible to recovered without going through the infectious state. We can implement this feature like this:

```
def add_immunization(system, fraction):
    system.init.s -= fraction
    system.init.r += fraction
```

add_immunization moves the given fraction of the population from S to R.

As a basis for comparison, let's run the model with the same parameters as in the previous chapter, with no immunization:

```
tc = 3 # time between contacts in days
tr = 4 # recovery time in days

beta = 1 / tc # contact rate (per day)
gamma = 1 / tr # recovery rate (per day)

system = make_system(beta, gamma)
results = run_simulation(system, update_func)
```

Now let's see what happens if 10 percent of students are immune. We will make another System object with the same parameters, and then we'll run add_immunization to modify the initial conditions:

```
system2 = make_system(beta, gamma)
add_immunization(system2, 0.1)
```

Now we can run the simulation like this:

```
results2 = run_simulation(system2, update_func)
```

The following figure shows s as a function of time, with and without immunization:

```
results.s.plot(style='--', label='No immunization')
results2.s.plot(label='10% immunization')

decorate(xlabel='Time (days)',
         ylabel='Fraction of population')
```

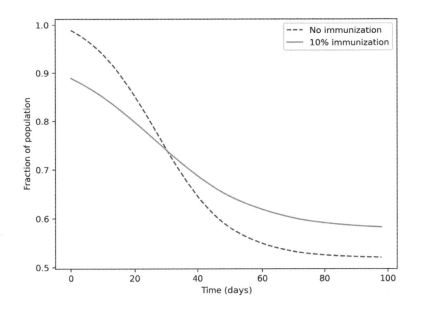

With immunization, there is a smaller change in s; that is, fewer people are infected. In the next section we'll compute this change and use it to quantify the effect of immunization.

Choosing Metrics

When we plot a time series, we get a view of everything that happened when the model ran, but often we want to boil it down to a few metrics that summarize the outcome.

In the KM model, we might want to know the time until the peak of the outbreak, the number of people who are sick at the peak, the number of students who will still be sick at the end of the semester, or the total number of students who get sick at any point. As an example, I will focus on the last one—the total number of sick students—and we will consider interventions intended to minimize it.

We can get the total number of infections by computing the difference in s at the beginning and the end of the simulation:

```
def calc_total_infected(results, system):
    s_0 = results.s[0]
    s_end = results.s[system.t_end]
    return s_0 - s_end
```

Here is the result from the first simulation:

```
calc_total_infected(results, system)
```

```
0.468320811028781
```

and from the second:

```
calc_total_infected(results2, system2)
```

```
0.30650802853979753
```

Without immunization, almost 47 percent of the population gets infected at some point. With 10 percent immunization, only 31 percent of the population gets infected. That's pretty good.

Sweeping Immunization

Now let's see what happens if we administer more vaccines. This following function sweeps a range of immunization rates:

```
def sweep_immunity(fraction_array):
    sweep = SweepSeries()

    for fraction in fraction_array:
        system = make_system(beta, gamma)
        add_immunization(system, fraction)
        results = run_simulation(system, update_func)
        sweep[fraction] = calc_total_infected(results, system)

    return sweep
```

The parameter of sweep_immunity is an array of immunization rates. The result is a SweepSeries object that maps from each immunization rate to the resulting fraction of students ever infected.

We can call it like this:

```
fraction_array = linspace(0, 1, 21)
infected_sweep = sweep_immunity(fraction_array)
```

The following figure plots the SweepSeries:

```
infected_sweep.plot(color='C2')

decorate(xlabel='Fraction immunized',
        ylabel='Total fraction infected',
        title='Fraction infected vs. immunization rate')
```

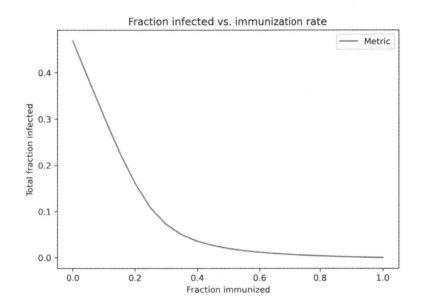

Notice that the x-axis is the immunization rate, not time.

As the immunization rate increases, the number of infections drops steeply. If 40 percent of the students are immunized, fewer than 4 percent get sick. That's because immunization has two effects: it protects the people who get immunized (of course) but it also protects the rest of the population.

Reducing the number of "susceptibles" and increasing the number of "resistants" makes it harder for the disease to spread, because some fraction of contacts are wasted on people who cannot be infected. This phenomenon is called *herd immunity*, and it is an important element of public health.

The steepness of the curve is a blessing and a curse. It's a blessing because it means we don't have to immunize everyone, and vaccines can protect the "herd" even if they are not 100 percent effective.

But it's a curse because a small decrease in immunization can cause a big increase in infections. In this example, if we drop from 80 percent immunization to 60 percent, that might not be too bad. But if we drop from 40 percent to 20 percent, that would trigger a major outbreak, affecting more than 15 percent of the population. For a serious disease like measles, just to name one, that would be a public health catastrophe.

Summary

In general, models are used to predict, explain, and design. In this chapter, we used an SIR model to predict the effect of immunization and to explain the phenomenon of herd immunity.

In the repository for this book, you will find a file called *plague.ipynb* that uses this model for design, that is, for making public health decisions intended to achieve a goal.

In the next chapter, we'll explore the SIR model further by sweeping the parameters.

Exercise

12.1

Suppose we have the option to quarantine infected students. For example, a student who feels ill might be moved to an infirmary or a private dorm room until they are no longer infectious. How might you incorporate the effect of quarantine in the SIR model?

13

SWEEPING PARAMETERS

In the previous chapter, we extended the Kermack-McKendrick (KM) model to include immunization and used it to demonstrate herd immunity. But we assumed that the parameters of the model, contact rate and recovery rate, were known. In this chapter, we'll explore the behavior of the model as we vary these parameters.

In the next chapter, we'll use analysis to understand these relationships better, and propose a method for using data to estimate parameters.

This chapter is available as a Jupyter notebook where you can read the text, run the code, and work on the exercise. You can access the notebooks at *https://allendowney.github.io/ModSimPy*.

Sweeping Beta

Recall that β is the contact rate, which captures both the frequency of interactions between people and the fraction of those interactions that result in a new infection. If N is the size of the population and s is the fraction that's susceptible, sN is the number of susceptibles, βsN is the number of contacts per day between susceptibles and other people, and βsiN is the number of those contacts where the other person is infectious.

As β increases, we expect the total number of infections to increase. To quantify that relationship, let's create a range of values for β:

```
beta_array = linspace(0.1, 1.1, 11)
gamma = 0.25
```

We'll start with a single value for gamma, which is the recovery rate, that is, the fraction of infected people who recover per day.

The following function takes beta_array and gamma as parameters:

```
def sweep_beta(beta_array, gamma):
    sweep = SweepSeries()
    for beta in beta_array:
        system = make_system(beta, gamma)
        results = run_simulation(system, update_func)
        sweep[beta] = calc_total_infected(results, system)
    return sweep
```

The function runs the simulation for each value of beta and computes the same metric we used in the previous chapter: the fraction of the population that gets infected. The result is a SweepSeries that contains the values of beta and the corresponding metrics.

We can run sweep_beta like this:

```
infected_sweep = sweep_beta(beta_array, gamma)
```

Before we plot the results, I will use a formatted string literal, also called an *f-string*, to assemble a label that includes the value of gamma:

```
label = f'gamma = {gamma}'
label
```
```
'gamma = 0.25'
```

An f-string starts with the letter f followed by a string in single or double quotes. The string can contain any number of format specifiers in squiggly brackets, {}. When a variable name appears in a format specifier, it is replaced with the value of the variable. In this example, the value of gamma is 0.25, so the value of label is 'gamma = 0.25'. You can read more about f-strings at *https://docs.python.org/3/tutorial/inputoutput.html#tut-f-strings*.

Now let's see the results:

```
infected_sweep.plot(label=label, color='C1')

decorate(xlabel='Contact rate (beta)',
         ylabel='Fraction infected')
```

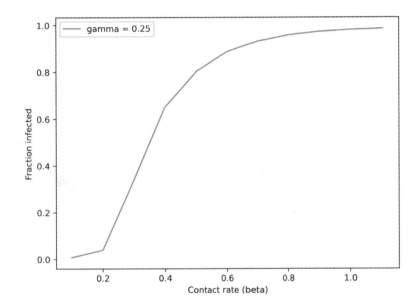

Remember that this figure is a parameter sweep, not a time series, so the *x*-axis is the parameter beta, not time.

When beta is small, the contact rate is low and the outbreak never really takes off; the total number of infected students is near zero. As beta increases, it reaches a threshold near 0.3 where the fraction of infected students increases quickly. When beta exceeds 0.5, more than 80 percent of the population gets sick.

Sweeping Gamma

Let's see what that looks like for a few different values of gamma. We'll use linspace to make an array of values:

```
gamma_array = linspace(0.1, 0.7, 4)
gamma_array
```

```
array([0.1, 0.3, 0.5, 0.7])
```

Then we'll run `sweep_beta` for each value of gamma:

```
for gamma in gamma_array:
    infected_sweep = sweep_beta(beta_array, gamma)
    label = f'gamma = {gamma}'
    infected_sweep.plot(label=label)

decorate(xlabel='Contact rate (beta)',
         ylabel='Fraction infected')
```

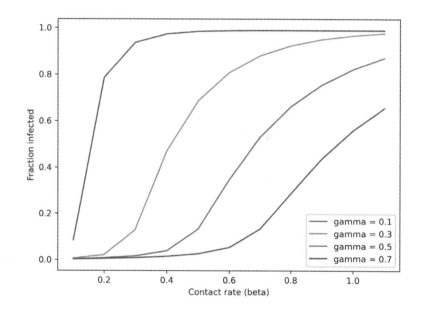

When gamma is low, the recovery rate is low, which means people are infectious longer. In that case, even a low contact rate (beta) results in an epidemic.

When gamma is high, beta has to be even higher to get things going.

Using a SweepFrame

In the previous section, we swept a range of values for gamma, and for each value of gamma we swept a range of values for beta. This process is a *two-dimensional sweep*.

If we want to store the results, rather than plot them, we can use a `SweepFrame` object, which is a kind of `DataFrame` where the rows sweep one parameter, the columns sweep another parameter, and the values contain metrics from a simulation.

This function shows how it works:

```
def sweep_parameters(beta_array, gamma_array):
    frame = SweepFrame(columns=gamma_array)
    for gamma in gamma_array:
        frame[gamma] = sweep_beta(beta_array, gamma)
    return frame
```

sweep_parameters takes as parameters an array of values for beta and an array of values for gamma. It creates a SweepFrame to store the results, with one column for each value of gamma and one row for each value of beta.

Each time through the loop, we run sweep_beta. The result is a SweepSeries object with one element for each value of beta. The assignment inside the loop stores the SweepSeries as a new column in the SweepFrame, corresponding to the current value of gamma.

At the end, the SweepFrame stores the fraction of students infected for each pair of parameters, beta and gamma.

We can run sweep_parameters like this:

```
frame = sweep_parameters(beta_array, gamma_array)
```

With the results in a SweepFrame, we can plot each column like this:

```
for gamma in gamma_array:
    label = f'gamma = {gamma}'
    frame[gamma].plot(label=label)

decorate(xlabel='Contact rate (beta)',
         ylabel='Fraction infected',
         title='Sweep beta, multiple values of gamma')
```

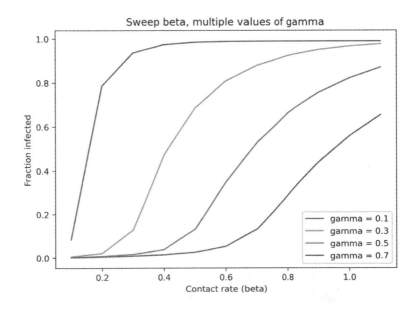

Alternatively, we can plot each row like this:

```
for beta in [0.2, 0.5, 0.8, 1.1]:
    label = f'beta = {beta}'
    frame.loc[beta].plot(label=label)

decorate(xlabel='Recovery rate (gamma)',
         ylabel='Fraction infected',
         title='Sweep gamma, multiple values of beta')
```

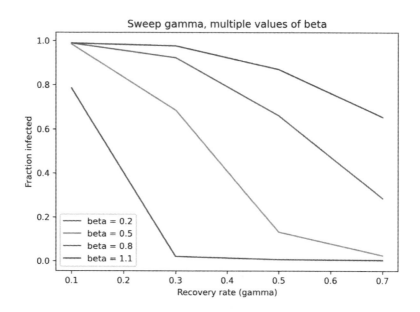

This example demonstrates one use of a SweepFrame: we can run the analysis once, save the results, and then generate different visualizations.

Another way to visualize the results of a two-dimensional sweep is a *contour plot*, which shows the parameters on the axes and contour lines where the value of the metric is constant. The ModSim library provides contour, which takes a SweepFrame and uses Matplotlib to generate a contour plot:

```
contour(frame)

decorate(xlabel='Recovery rate (gamma)',
         ylabel='Contact rate (beta)',
         title='Contour plot, fraction infected')
```

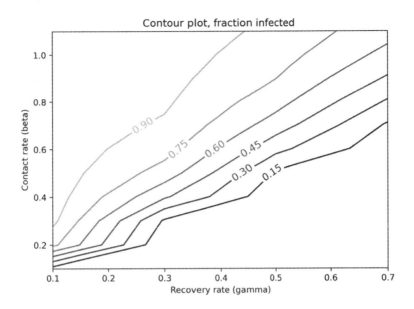

Contour plot, fraction infected

The values of gamma are on the x-axis, corresponding to the columns of the SweepFrame. The values of beta are on the y-axis, corresponding to the rows of the SweepFrame. Each line follows a contour where the infection rate is constant.

Infection rates are lowest in the lower right, where the contact rate is low and the recovery rate is high. They increase as we move to the upper left, where the contact rate is high and the recovery rate is low.

Summary

This chapter demonstrated a two-dimensional parameter sweep using a SweepFrame to store the results.

We plotted the results three ways:

- First we plotted total infections versus beta, with one line for each value of gamma.

- Then we plotted total infections versus gamma, with one line for each value of beta.

- Finally, we made a contour plot with beta on the y-axis, gamma on the x-axis, and contour lines where the metric is constant.

These visualizations suggest that there is a relationship between beta and gamma that determines the outcome of the model. In fact, there is. In the next chapter we'll explore it by running simulations, then derive it by analysis.

Exercise

13.1

If we know beta and gamma, we can compute the fraction of the population that gets infected. In general, we don't know these parameters, but sometimes we can estimate them based on the behavior of an outbreak.

Suppose the infectious period for the Freshman Plague is known to be two days on average, and suppose during one particularly bad year 40 percent of the class is infected at some point. Estimate the time between contacts, 1/beta.

14

NONDIMENSIONALIZATION

In the previous chapter, we swept the parameters of the Kermack-McKendrick (KM) model: the contact rate, beta, and the recovery rate, gamma. For each pair of parameters, we ran a simulation and computed the total fraction of the population infected.

In this chapter, we'll investigate the relationship between the parameters and this metric, using both simulation and analysis.

This chapter is available as a Jupyter notebook where you can read the text, run the code, and work on the exercises. You can access the notebooks at *https://allendowney.github.io/ModSimPy*.

Beta and Gamma

The figures in the previous chapter suggest that there is a relationship between the parameters of the KM model, beta and gamma, and the fraction of the population that is infected. Let's think what that relationship might be.

- When beta exceeds gamma, there are more contacts than recoveries during each day. The difference between beta and gamma might be called the *excess contact rate*, in units of contacts per day.

- As an alternative, we might consider the ratio beta/gamma, which is the number of contacts per recovery. Because the numerator and denominator are in the same units, this ratio is *dimensionless*, which means it has no units.

Describing physical systems using dimensionless parameters is often a useful move in the modeling and simulation game. In fact, it is so useful that it has a name: *nondimensionalization*. So that's what we'll try first.

Exploring the Results

In the previous chapter, we wrote a function, sweep_parameters, that takes an array of values for beta and an array of values for gamma. It runs a simulation for each pair of parameters and returns a SweepFrame with the results.

Let's run it again with the following arrays of parameters:

```
beta_array = [0.1, 0.2, 0.3, 0.4, 0.5,
              0.6, 0.7, 0.8, 0.9, 1.0, 1.1]
gamma_array = [0.2, 0.4, 0.6, 0.8]
frame = sweep_parameters(beta_array, gamma_array)
```

Here's what the first few rows look like:

```
frame.head()
```

Parameter	0.2	0.4	0.6	0.8
0.1	0.010756	0.003642	0.002191	0.001567
0.2	0.118984	0.010763	0.005447	0.003644
0.3	0.589095	0.030185	0.010771	0.006526
0.4	0.801339	0.131563	0.020917	0.010780
0.5	0.896577	0.396409	0.046140	0.017640

The SweepFrame has one row for each value of beta and one column for each value of gamma. We can print the values in the SweepFrame like this:

```
for gamma in frame.columns:
    column = frame[gamma]
    for beta in column.index:
        metric = column[beta]
        print(beta, gamma, metric)
```

```
0.1 0.2 0.010756340768063644
0.2 0.2 0.11898421353185373
0.3 0.2 0.5890954199973404
--snip--
0.9 0.8 0.2668895539427739
1.0 0.8 0.40375121210421994
1.1 0.8 0.519583469821867
```

This is the first example we've seen with one for loop inside another:

- Each time the outer loop runs, it selects a value of gamma from the columns of the SweepFrame and extracts the corresponding column.

- Each time the inner loop runs, it selects a value of beta from the index of the column and selects the corresponding element, which is the fraction of the population that got infected.

Since there are 11 rows and 4 columns, the total number of lines in the output is 44.

The following function uses the same loops to enumerate the elements of the SweepFrame, but instead of printing a line for each element, it plots a point:

```
from matplotlib.pyplot import plot

def plot_sweep_frame(frame):
    for gamma in frame.columns:
        column = frame[gamma]
        for beta in column.index:
            metric = column[beta]
            plot(beta/gamma, metric, '.', color='C1')
```

For each element of the SweepFrame it plots a point with the ratio beta/gamma as the x-coordinate and metric—which is the fraction of the population that's infected—as the y-coordinate.

Here's what it looks like:

```
plot_sweep_frame(frame)

decorate(xlabel='Contact number (beta/gamma)',
         ylabel='Fraction infected')
```

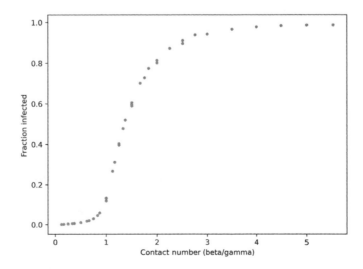

The results fall on a single curve, at least approximately. That means that we can predict the fraction of the population that will be infected based on a single parameter, the ratio beta/gamma. We don't need to know the values of beta and gamma separately.

Contact Number

From Chapter 11, recall that the number of new infections in a given day is $\beta si N$, and the number of recoveries is $\gamma i N$. If we divide these quantities, the result is $\beta s/\gamma$, which is the number of new infections per recovery (as a fraction of the population).

When a new disease is introduced to a susceptible population, s is approximately 1, so the number of people infected by each sick person is β/γ. This ratio is called the *contact number* or *basic reproduction number*. By convention it is usually denoted R_0, but in the context of an SIR model, that notation is confusing, so we'll use c instead.

The results in the previous section suggest that there is a relationship between c and the total number of infections. We can derive this relationship by analyzing the differential equations from Chapter 11:

$$\frac{ds}{dt} = -\beta si$$

$$\frac{di}{dt} = \beta si - \gamma i$$

$$\frac{dr}{dt} = \gamma i$$

In the same way we divided the contact rate by the infection rate to get the dimensionless quantity c, now we'll divide di/dt by ds/dt to get a ratio of rates:

$$\frac{di}{ds} = \frac{\beta si - \gamma i}{-\beta si}$$

which we can simplify as:

$$\frac{di}{ds} = -1 + \frac{\gamma}{\beta s}$$

Replacing β/γ with c, we can write:

$$\frac{di}{ds} = -1 + \frac{1}{cs}$$

Dividing one differential equation by another is not an obvious move, but in this case it is useful because it gives us a relationship between i, s, and c that does not depend on time. From that relationship, we can derive an equation that relates c to the final value of s. In theory, this equation makes it possible to infer c by observing the course of an epidemic.

Here's how the derivation goes. We multiply both sides of the previous equation by ds:

$$di = \left(-1 + \frac{1}{cs}\right) ds$$

and then integrate both sides:

$$i = -s + \frac{1}{c} \log s + q$$

where q is a constant of integration. Rearranging terms yields:

$$q = i + s - \frac{1}{c} \log s$$

Now let's see if we can figure out what q is. At the beginning of an epidemic, if the fraction infected is small and nearly everyone is susceptible, we can use the approximations $i(0) = 0$ and $s(0) = 1$ to compute q:

$$q = 0 + 1 + \frac{1}{c} \log 1$$

Since $\log 1 = 0$, we get $q = 1$.

Now, at the end of the epidemic, let's assume that $i(\infty) = 0$, and $s(\infty)$ is an unknown quantity, s_∞. Now we have:

$$q = 1 = 0 + s_\infty - \frac{1}{c} \log s_\infty$$

Solving for c, we get:

$$c = \frac{\log s_\infty}{s_\infty - 1}$$

By relating c and s_∞, this equation makes it possible to estimate c based on data, and possibly predict the behavior of future epidemics.

Comparing Analysis and Simulation

Let's compare this analytic result to the results from simulation. We'll create an array of values for s_∞:

```
s_inf_array = linspace(0.003, 0.99, 50)
```

and compute the corresponding values of c:

```
from numpy import log

c_array = log(s_inf_array) / (s_inf_array - 1)
```

To get the total infected, we compute the difference between $s(0)$ and $s(\infty)$, then store the results in a Series:

```
frac_infected = 1 - s_inf_array
```

The ModSim library provides a function called make_series we can use to put c_array and frac_infected in a pandas Series:

```
frac_infected_series = make_series(c_array, frac_infected)
```

Now we can plot the results:

```
plot_sweep_frame(frame)
frac_infected_series.plot(label='analysis')

decorate(xlabel='Contact number (c)',
         ylabel='Fraction infected')
```

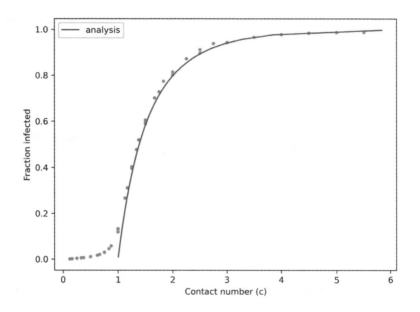

When the contact number exceeds 1, analysis and simulation agree. When the contact number is less than 1, they do not: analysis indicates there should be no infections; in the simulations there are a small number of infections.

The reason for the discrepancy is that the simulation divides time into a discrete series of days, whereas the analysis treats time as a continuous quantity. When the contact number is large, these two models agree; when it is small, they diverge.

Estimating the Contact Number

The previous figure shows that if we know the contact number, we can estimate the fraction of the population that will be infected with just a few arithmetic operations. We don't have to run a simulation.

We can also read the figure the other way; if we know what fraction of the population was affected by a past outbreak, we can estimate the contact number. Then, if we know one of the parameters, like gamma, we can use the contact number to estimate the other parameter, like beta.

At least, in theory we can. In practice, it might not work very well, because of the shape of the curve:

- When the contact number is low, the curve is quite steep, which means that small changes in c yield big changes in the number of infections. If we observe that the total fraction infected is anywhere from 20 percent to 80 percent, we would conclude that c is near 2.

- When the contact number is high, the curve is nearly flat, which means that it's hard to see the difference between values of c between 3 and 6.

With the uncertainty of real data, we might not be able to estimate c with much precision. But as one of the exercises below, you'll have a chance to try.

Summary

In this chapter we used simulations to explore the relationship between beta, gamma, and the fraction infected. Then we used analysis to explain that relationship.

With that, we are done with the Kermack-McKendrick model. In the next chapter, we'll move on to thermal systems and the notorious coffee cooling problem.

Exercises

14.1

At the beginning of this chapter, I suggested two ways to relate beta and gamma: we could compute their difference or their ratio.

Because the ratio is dimensionless, I suggested we explore it first, and that led us to discover the contact number, which is beta/gamma. When we plotted the fraction infected as a function of the contact number, we found that this metric falls on a single curve, at least approximately. That indicates that the ratio is enough to predict the results; we don't have to know beta and gamma individually.

But that leaves a question open: what happens if we do the same thing using the difference instead of the ratio?

Write a version of plot_sweep_frame, called plot_sweep_frame_difference, that plots the fraction infected versus the difference beta-gamma.

What do the results look like, and what does that imply?

14.2

Suppose you run a survey at the end of the semester and find that 26 percent of students had the Freshman Plague at some point. What is your best estimate of c?

Hint: If you display frac_infected_series, you can read off the answer.

14.3

So far the only metric we have considered is the total fraction of the population that gets infected over the course of an epidemic. That is an important metric, but it is not the only one we care about.

For example, if we have limited resources to deal with infected people, we might also be concerned about the number of people who are sick at the peak of the epidemic, which is the maximum of I.

Write a version of `sweep_beta` that computes this metric, and use it to compute a `SweepFrame` for a range of values of `beta` and `gamma`. Make a contour plot that shows the value of this metric as a function of `beta` and `gamma`.

Then use `plot_sweep_frame` to plot the maximum of I as a function of the contact number, `beta/gamma`. Do the results fall on a single curve?

Under the Hood

ModSim provides `make_series` to make it easier to create a pandas `Series`. In this chapter, we used it like this:

```
frac_infected_series = make_series(c_array, frac_infected)
```

If you import `Series` from pandas, you can make a `Series` yourself, like this:

```
from pandas import Series

frac_infected_series = Series(frac_infected, c_array)
```

The difference is that the arguments are in reverse order: the first argument is stored as the values in the `Series`; the second argument is stored as the index.

I find that order counterintuitive, which is why I use `make_series`. `make_series` takes the same optional arguments as `Series`, which you can read about at *https://pandas.pydata.org/pandas-docs/stable/reference/api/ pandas.Series.html*.

15

THERMAL SYSTEMS

So far the systems we have studied have been physical in the sense that they exist in the world, but they have not been physics in the sense of what physics classes are usually about. In the next few chapters, we'll do some physics, starting with *thermal systems*, that is, systems where the temperature of objects changes as heat transfers from one to another.

This chapter is available as a Jupyter notebook where you can read the text, run the code, and work on the exercises. You can access the notebooks at *https://allendowney.github.io/ModSimPy*.

The Coffee Cooling Problem

The coffee cooling problem was discussed by Jearl Walker in "The Amateur Scientist," published in the November 1977 issue of *Scientific American*. Since then it has become a standard example of modeling and simulation.

Here is my version of the problem:

> Suppose I stop on the way to work to pick up a cup of coffee and a small container of milk. Assuming that I want the coffee to be as hot as possible when I arrive at work, should I add the milk at the coffee shop, wait until I get to work, or add the milk at some point in between?

To help answer this question, I made a trial run with the milk and coffee in separate containers and took some measurements (not really):

- When served, the temperature of the coffee is 90°C. The volume is 300 mL.

- The milk is at an initial temperature of 5°C, and I take about 50 mL.

- The ambient temperature in my car is 22°C.

- The coffee is served in a well-insulated cup. When I arrive at work after 30 minutes, the temperature of the coffee has fallen to 70°C.

- The milk container is not as well insulated. After 15 minutes, it warms up to 20°C, nearly the ambient temperature.

To use this data and answer the question, we have to know something about temperature and heat, and we have to make some modeling decisions.

Temperature and Heat

To understand how coffee cools (and milk warms), we need a model of temperature and heat. *Temperature* is a property of an object or a system; in SI units it is measured in degrees Celsius (°C). Temperature quantifies how hot or cold the object is, which is related to the average velocity of the particles that make it up.

When particles in a hot object contact particles in a cold object, the hot object gets cooler and the cold object gets warmer as energy is transferred from one to the other. The transferred energy is called *heat*; in SI units it is measured in joules (J).

Heat is related to temperature by the following equation:

$$Q = C \Delta T$$

where Q is the amount of heat transferred to an object, ΔT is the resulting change in temperature, and C is the object's *thermal mass*, which is a property of the object that determines how much energy it takes to heat or cool it. In SI units, thermal mass is measured in joules per degree Celsius (J/°C).

For objects made primarily from one material, thermal mass can be computed like this:

$$C = mc_p$$

where m is the mass of the object and c_p is the *specific heat capacity* of the material, which is the amount of thermal mass per gram.

We can use these equations to estimate the thermal mass of a cup of coffee. The specific heat capacity of coffee is probably close to that of water, which is 4.2 J/g/°C. Assuming that the density of coffee is close to that of water, which is 1 g/mL, the mass of 300 mL of coffee is 300 g, and the thermal mass is 1,260 J/°C.

So when a cup of coffee cools from 90°C to 70°C, the change in temperature, ΔT, is 20°C, which means that 25,200 J of heat energy was transferred from the cup and the coffee to the surrounding environment (the cup holder and air in my car).

To give you a sense of how much energy that is, if you were able to harness all of that heat to do work (which you cannot), you could use it to lift a cup of coffee from sea level to 8,571 m, just shy of the height of Mount Everest, 8,848 m.

Heat Transfer

In a situation like the coffee cooling problem, there are three ways heat transfers from one object to another:

Conduction   When objects at different temperatures come into contact, the faster-moving particles of the higher-temperature object transfer kinetic energy to the slower-moving particles of the lower-temperature object.

Convection   When particles in a gas or liquid flow from place to place, they carry heat energy with them. Fluid flows can be caused by external action, like stirring, or by internal differences in temperature. For example, you might have heard that hot air rises, which is a form of "natural convection."

Radiation   As the particles in an object move due to thermal energy, they emit electromagnetic radiation. The energy carried by this radiation depends on the object's temperature and surface properties.

For objects like coffee in a car, the effect of radiation is much smaller than the effects of conduction and convection, so we will ignore it.

Convection can be a complex topic, since it often depends on details of fluid flow in three dimensions. But for this problem we will be able to get away with a simple model called "Newton's law of cooling."

Newton's Law of Cooling

Newton's law of cooling asserts that the temperature rate of change for an object is proportional to the difference in temperature between the object and the surrounding environment:

$$\frac{dT}{dt} = -r(T - T_{env})$$

where t is time, T is the temperature of the object, T_{env} is the temperature of the environment, and r is a constant that characterizes how quickly heat is transferred between the object and the environment.

Newton's "law" is really a model: it is a good approximation in some conditions and less good in others. For example, if the primary mechanism of heat transfer is conduction, Newton's law is "true," which is to say that r is constant over a wide range of temperatures. And sometimes we can estimate r based on the material properties and shape of the object.

When convection contributes a non-negligible fraction of heat transfer, r depends on temperature, but Newton's law is often accurate enough, at least over a narrow range of temperatures. In this case r usually has to be estimated experimentally, since it depends on details of surface shape, air flow, evaporation, and so on.

When radiation makes up a substantial part of heat transfer, Newton's law is not a good model at all. This is the case for objects in space or in a vacuum, and for objects at high temperatures (more than a few hundred degrees Celsius, say). However, for a situation like the coffee cooling problem, we expect Newton's model to be quite good.

With that, we have just one more modeling decision to make: whether to treat the coffee and the cup as separate objects or a single object. If the cup is made of paper, it has less mass than the coffee, and the specific heat capacity of paper is lower, too. In that case, it would be reasonable to treat the cup and coffee as a single object. For a cup with substantial thermal mass, like a ceramic mug, we might consider a model that computes the temperature of coffee and cup separately.

Implementing Newtonian Cooling

To get started, we'll focus on the coffee. Then, as an exercise, you can simulate the milk. In the next chapter, we'll put them together, literally.

Here's a function that takes the parameters of the system and makes a System object:

```
def make_system(T_init, volume, r, t_end):
    return System(T_init=T_init,
                  T_final=T_init,
                  volume=volume,
                  r=r,
                  t_end=t_end,
                  T_env=22,
                  t_0=0,
                  dt=1)
```

In addition to the parameters, make_system sets the temperature of the environment, T_env, the initial timestamp, t_0, and the time step, dt, which we will use to simulate the cooling process.

Here's a System object that represents the coffee:

```
coffee = make_system(T_init=90, volume=300, r=0.01, t_end=30)
```

The values of T_init, volume, and t_end come from the statement of the problem. I chose the value of r arbitrarily for now; we will see how to estimate it soon.

Strictly speaking, Newton's law is a differential equation, but over a short period of time we can approximate it with a difference equation:

$$\Delta T = -r(T - T_{env}) dt$$

where dt is the time step and ΔT is the change in temperature during that time step.

NOTE *I use ΔT to denote a change in temperature over time, but in the context of heat transfer, you might also see ΔT used to denote the difference in temperature between an object and its environment, $T - T_{env}$. To minimize confusion, I avoid this second use.*

The following function takes the current time t, the current temperature T, and a System object and computes the change in temperature during a time step:

```
def change_func(t, T, system):
    r, T_env, dt = system.r, system.T_env, system.dt
    return -r * (T - T_env) * dt
```

We can test it with the initial temperature of the coffee, like this:

```
change_func(0, coffee.T_init, coffee)
```
```
-0.68
```

With dt=1 minute, the temperature drops by about 0.7°C, at least for this value of r.

Now here's a version of run_simulation that simulates a series of time steps from t_0 to t_end:

```
def run_simulation(system, change_func):
    t_array = linrange(system.t_0, system.t_end, system.dt)
    n = len(t_array)

    series = TimeSeries(index=t_array)
    series.iloc[0] = system.T_init

    for i in range(n-1):
        t = t_array[i]
        T = series.iloc[i]
        series.iloc[i+1] = T + change_func(t, T, system)

    system.T_final = series.iloc[-1]
    return series
```

There are two things here that are different from previous versions of run_simulation.

First, we use linrange to make an array of values from t_0 to t_end with time step dt. linrange is similar to linspace; they both take a start value and an end value and return an array of equally spaced values. The difference is the third argument: linspace takes an integer that indicates the number of points in the range; linrange takes a step size that indicates the interval between values. When we make the TimeSeries, we use the keyword argument index to indicate that the index of the TimeSeries is the array of timestamps, t_array.

Second, this version of run_simulation uses iloc rather than loc to specify the rows in the TimeSeries. Here's the difference:

- With loc, the label in square brackets can be any kind of value, with any start, end, and time step. For example, in the world population model, the labels are years starting in 1950 and ending in 2016.

- With iloc, the label in square brackets is always an integer starting at 0. So we can always get the first element with iloc[0] and the last element with iloc[-1], regardless of what the labels are.

In this version of run_simulation, the loop variable is an integer, i, that goes from 0 to n-1, including 0 but not including n-1. So the first time through the loop, i is 0 and the value we add to the TimeSeries has index 1. The last time through the loop, i is n-2 and the value we add has index n-1.

We can run the simulation like this:

```
results = run_simulation(coffee, change_func)
```

The result is a TimeSeries with one row per time step. Here are the first few rows:

```
show(results.head())
```

Time	Quantity
0.0	90.000000
1.0	89.320000
2.0	88.646800
3.0	87.980332
4.0	87.320529

and the last few rows:

```
show(results.tail())
```

Time	Quantity
26.0	74.362934
27.0	73.839305
28.0	73.320912
29.0	72.807702
30.0	72.299625

With t_0=0, t_end=30, and dt=1, the timestamps go from 0.0 to 30.0.
Here's what the TimeSeries looks like:

```
results.plot(label='coffee')

decorate(xlabel='Time (min)',
         ylabel='Temperature (C)',
         title='Coffee Cooling')
```

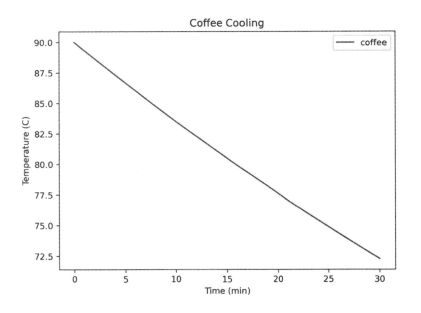

The temperature after 30 minutes is 72.3°C, which is a little higher than the measurement we're trying to match, which is 70°C:

```
coffee.T_final
```
```
72.2996253904031
```

To find the value of r where the final temperature is precisely 70°C, we could proceed by trial and error, but it is more efficient to use a root-finding algorithm.

Finding Roots

The ModSim library provides a function called root_scalar that finds the roots of nonlinear equations. As an example, suppose you want to find the roots of the following polynomial:

$$f(x) = (x-1)(x-2)(x-3)$$

A *root* is a value of x that makes $f(x) = 0$. Because of the way I wrote this polynomial, we can see that if $x = 1$, the first factor is 0; if $x = 2$, the second factor is 0; and if $x = 3$, the third factor is 0, so those are the roots.

I'll use this example to demonstrate root_scalar. First, we have to write a function that evaluates *f*:

```
def func(x):
    return (x-1) * (x-2) * (x-3)
```

Now we call root_scalar like this:

```
res = root_scalar(func, bracket=[1.5, 2.5])
res
```
```
     converged: True
          flag: 'converged'
function_calls: 3
    iterations: 2
          root: 2.0
```

The first argument is the function whose roots we want. The second argument is an interval that contains or *brackets* a root. The result is an object that contains several variables, including the Boolean value converged, which is True if the search converged successfully on a root, and root, which is the root that was found:

```
res.root
```
```
2.0
```

If we provide a different interval, we find a different root:

```
res = root_scalar(func, bracket=[2.5, 3.5])
res.root
```
```
2.9999771663211003
```

If the interval doesn't contain a root, you'll get a ValueError and a message like f(a) and f(b) must have different signs.

Now we can use root_scalar to estimate r.

Estimating r

What we want is the value of r that yields a final temperature of 70°C. To use root_scalar, we need a function that takes r as a parameter and returns the difference between the final temperature and the goal:

```
def error_func(r, system):
    system.r = r
    results = run_simulation(system, change_func)
    return system.T_final - 70
```

This is called an *error function* because it returns the difference between what we got and what we wanted, that is, the error. With the right value of r, the error is 0.

We can test error_func like this, using the initial guess r=0.01:

```
coffee = make_system(T_init=90, volume=300, r=0.01, t_end=30)
error_func(0.01, coffee)
```

```
2.2996253904030937
```

The result is an error of 2.3°C, which means the final temperature with r=0.01 is too high:

```
error_func(0.02, coffee)
```

```
-10.907066281994297
```

With r=0.02, the error is about −11°C, which means that the final temperature is too low. So we know that the correct value must be in between.

Now we can call root_scalar like this:

```
res = root_scalar(error_func, coffee, bracket=[0.01, 0.02])
res
```

```
      converged: True
           flag: 'converged'
 function_calls: 6
     iterations: 5
           root: 0.011543084190599507
```

The first argument is the error function. The second argument is the System object, which root_scalar passes as an argument to error_func. The third argument is an interval that brackets the root.

Here's the root we found:

```
r_coffee = res.root
r_coffee
```

0.011543084190599507

In this example, r_coffee turns out to be about 0.0115, in units of min^{-1} (inverse minutes).

We can confirm that this value is correct by setting r to the root we found and running the simulation:

```
coffee.r = res.root
run_simulation(coffee, change_func)
coffee.T_final
```

70.00000057308064

The final temperature is very close to 70°C.

Summary

This chapter presents the basics of heat, temperature, and Newton's law of cooling, which is a model that is accurate when most heat transfer is by conduction and convection, not radiation.

To simulate a hot cup of coffee, we wrote Newton's law as a difference equation, then wrote a version of run_simulation that implements it. Then we used root_scalar to find the value of r that matches the measurement from my hypothetical experiment.

All that is the first step toward solving the coffee cooling problem I posed at the beginning of the chapter. As an exercise, you'll do the next step, which is simulating the milk. In the next chapter, we'll model the mixing process and finish off the problem.

Exercises

15.1

Simulate the temperature of 50 mL of milk with a starting temperature of 5°C, in a vessel with r=0.1, for 15 minutes, and plot the results. Use make_system to make a System object that represents the milk, and use run_simulation to simulate it. By trial and error, find a value for r that makes the final temperature close to 20°C.

15.2

Write an error function that simulates the temperature of the milk and returns the difference between the final temperature and 20°C. Use it to estimate the value of r for the milk.

16

SOLVING THE COFFEE PROBLEM

In the previous chapter, we wrote a simulation of a cooling cup of coffee. Given the initial temperature of the coffee, the temperature of the atmosphere, and the rate parameter, r, we predicted the temperature of the coffee over time. Then we used a root-finding algorithm to estimate r based on data. If you did the exercises, you simulated the temperature of the milk as it warmed, and estimated its rate parameter as well.

Now let's put it together. In this chapter we'll write a function that simulates mixing the two liquids, and use it to answer the question we started with: Is it better to mix the coffee and milk at the beginning, the end, or somewhere in the middle?

This chapter is available as a Jupyter notebook where you can read the text, run the code, and work on the exercises. You can access the notebooks at *https://allendowney.github.io/ModSimPy*.

Mixing Liquids

When we mix two liquids, the temperature of the mixture depends on the temperatures of the ingredients, as well as their volumes, densities, and specific heat capacities (as defined in the previous chapter). In this section I'll explain how to calculate the temperature of the mixture.

Assuming there are no chemical reactions that either produce or consume heat, the total thermal energy of the system is the same before and after mixing; in other words, thermal energy is *conserved*.

If the temperature of the first liquid is T_1, the temperature of the second liquid is T_2, and the final temperature of the mixture is T, then the heat transfer into the first liquid is $C_1(T - T_1)$ and the heat transfer into the second liquid is $C_2(T - T_2)$, where C_1 and C_2 are the thermal masses of the liquids.

In order to conserve energy, these heat transfers must add up to 0:

$$C_1(T - T_1) + C_2(T - T_2) = 0$$

We can solve this equation for T:

$$T = \frac{C_1 T_1 + C_2 T_2}{C_1 + C_2}$$

For the coffee cooling problem, we have the volume of each liquid; if we also know the density, ρ, and the specific heat capacity, c_p, we can compute thermal mass:

$$C = \rho V c_p$$

If the liquids have the same density and heat capacity, they drop out of the equation, and we can write:

$$T = \frac{V_1 T_1 + V_2 T_2}{V_1 + V_2}$$

where V_1 and V_2 are the volumes of the liquids.

As an approximation, let's assume that milk and coffee have the same density and specific heat. If you are interested, you can look up these quantities and see how good this assumption is.

Now let's simulate the mixing process. The following function takes two System objects, representing the coffee and milk, and creates a new System to represent the mixture:

```
def mix(system1, system2):

    V1, V2 = system1.volume, system2.volume
    T1, T2 = system1.T_final, system2.T_final

    V_mix = V1 + V2
    T_mix = (V1 * T1 + V2 * T2) / V_mix
```

```
        return make_system(T_init=T_mix,
                            volume=V_mix,
                            r=system1.r,
                            t_end=30)
```

The first two lines extract volume and temperature from the System objects. The next two lines compute the volume and temperature of the mixture. Finally, mix makes a new System object and returns it.

This function uses the value of r from system1 as the value of r for the mixture. If system1 represents the coffee, and we are adding the milk to the coffee, this is probably a reasonable choice. On the other hand, when we increase the amount of liquid in the coffee cup, that might change r. So this is an assumption we might want to revisit.

Now we have everything we need to solve the problem.

Mix First or Last?

First let's create objects to represent the coffee and milk. For r_coffee, we'll use the value we computed in the previous chapter:

```
r_coffee = 0.0115
coffee = make_system(T_init=90, volume=300, r=r_coffee, t_end=30)
```

For r_milk, we'll use the value I estimated for Exercise 15.2 in the previous chapter:

```
r_milk = 0.133
milk = make_system(T_init=5, volume=50, r=r_milk, t_end=15)
```

Now we can mix them and simulate 30 minutes:

```
mix_first = mix(coffee, milk)
run_simulation(mix_first, change_func)

mix_first.T_final
```
```
61.48016207445017
```

The final temperature is 61.5°C, which is still warm enough to be enjoyable. Would we do any better if we added the milk last?

Let's simulate the coffee and milk separately, and then mix them:

```
run_simulation(coffee, change_func)
run_simulation(milk, change_func)
mix_last = mix(coffee, milk)
mix_last.T_final
```
```
62.91117032872072
```

After mixing, the temperature is 62.9°C, so it looks like adding the milk at the end is better. But is that the best we can do?

Optimal Timing

Adding the milk after 30 minutes is better than adding it immediately, but maybe there's something in between that's even better. To find out, let's use the following function, which takes the time to add the milk, t_add, as a parameter:

```
def run_and_mix(t_add, t_total):
    coffee.t_end = t_add
    coffee_results = run_simulation(coffee, change_func)

    milk.t_end = t_add
    milk_results = run_simulation(milk, change_func)

    mixture = mix(coffee, milk)
    mixture.t_end = t_total - t_add
    results = run_simulation(mixture, change_func)

    return mixture.T_final
```

run_and_mix simulates both systems for the given time, t_add. Then it mixes them and simulates the mixture for the remaining time, t_total - t_add.

When t_add is 0, we add the milk immediately; when t_add is 30, we add it at the end. Now we can sweep the range of values in between:

```
sweep = SweepSeries()
for t_add in linspace(0, 30, 11):
    sweep[t_add] = run_and_mix(t_add, 30)
```

Here's what the results look like:

```
sweep.plot(label='mixture', color='C2')

decorate(xlabel='Time until mixing (min)',
         ylabel='Final temperature (C)')
```

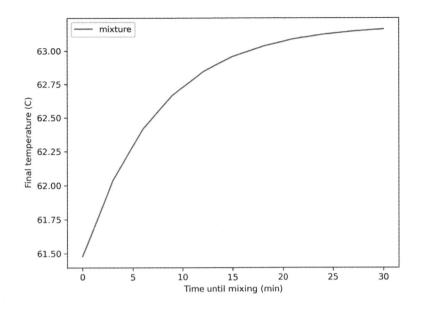

Note that this is a parameter sweep, not a time series.

The final temperature is maximized when t_add=30, so adding the milk at the end is optimal.

The Analytic Solution

Simulating Newton's law of cooling isn't really necessary because we can solve the differential equation analytically. If

$$\frac{dT}{dt} = -r(T - T_{env})$$

the general solution is

$$T(t) = C\exp(-rt) + T_{env}$$

and the particular solution where $T(0) = T_{init}$ is

$$T_{env} + \left(-T_{env} + T_{init}\right)\exp(-rt)$$

Now we can use the observed data to estimate the parameter r. If we observe that the temperature at t_{end} is T_{final}, we can plug these values into the particular solution and solve for r. The result is:

$$r = \frac{1}{t_{end}} \log\left(\frac{T_{init} - T_{env}}{T_{final} - T_{env}}\right)$$

The following function takes a System object and computes r:

```
from numpy import log

def compute_r(system):
    t_end = system.t_end
    T_init = system.T_init
    T_final = system.T_final
    T_env = system.T_env

    r = log((T_init - T_env) / (T_final - T_env)) / t_end
    return r
```

We can use this function to compute r for the coffee, given the parameters of the problem:

```
coffee2 = make_system(T_init=90, volume=300, r=0, t_end=30)
coffee2.T_final = 70
r_coffee2 = compute_r(coffee2)
r_coffee2
```

```
0.01161022314227386
```

This value is close to the value of r we computed in the previous chapter, 0.115, but not exactly the same. That's because the simulations use discrete time steps, and the analysis uses continuous time.

Nevertheless, the results of the analysis are consistent with the simulation. To check, we'll use the following function, which takes a System object and uses the analytic result to compute a time series:

```
from numpy import exp

def run_analysis(system):
    T_env, T_init, r = system.T_env, system.T_init, system.r

    t_array = linrange(system.t_0, system.t_end, system.dt)
    T_array = T_env + (T_init - T_env) * exp(-r * t_array)

    system.T_final = T_array[-1]
    return make_series(t_array, T_array)
```

The first line unpacks the system variables. The next two lines compute t_array, which is a NumPy array of timestamps, and T_array, which is an array of the corresponding temperatures. The last two lines store the final temperature in the System object and use make_series to return the results in a pandas Series.

We can run it like this:

```
coffee2.r = r_coffee2
results2 = run_analysis(coffee2)
coffee2.T_final
```

70.0

The final temperature is 70°C, as it should be. In fact, the results are almost identical to what we got by simulation, with a small difference due to rounding.

Since we can solve this problem analytically, you might wonder why we bothered writing a simulation. One reason is validation: since we solved the same problem in two ways, we can be more confident that the answer is correct. The other reason is flexibility: now that we have a working simulation, it would be easy to add more features. For example, the temperature of the environment might change over time, or we could simulate the coffee and container as two objects. If the coffee and milk are next to each other, we could include the heat flow between them. A model with these features would be difficult or impossible to solve analytically.

Summary

In this chapter we finished the coffee cooling problem from the previous chapter and found that it is better to add the milk at the end, at least for the version of the problem I posed. As an exercise you will have a chance to explore a variation of the problem where the answer might be different.

In the next chapter, we'll move on to a new example, a model of how glucose and insulin interact to control blood sugar.

Exercises

16.1

Use compute_r to compute r_milk according to the analytic solution. Run the analysis with this value of r_milk and confirm that the results are consistent with the simulation.

16.2

Suppose the coffee shop won't let me take milk in a separate container, but I keep a bottle of milk in the refrigerator at my office. In that case is it better to add the milk at the coffee shop or wait until I get to the office?

Hint: Think about the simplest way to represent the behavior of a refrigerator in this model. The change you make to test this variation of the problem should be very small!

17

MODELING BLOOD SUGAR

In this chapter, we'll start a new example, a model of how glucose and insulin interact to control blood sugar. We will implement a widely used model called the minimal model because it is intended to include only the elements essential to explain the observed behavior of the system. Here we'll present the model and some background information we need to understand it. In the next chapter we'll implement the model and compare the results to real data.

My presentation in this chapter follows R. N. Bergman's paper "Minimal Model: Perspective," published in 2005 in *Hormone Research in Pediatrics* (see *https://www.karger.com/article/Abstract/89312*).

This chapter is available as a Jupyter notebook where you can read the text, run the code, and work on the exercises. You can access the notebooks at *https://allendowney.github.io/ModSimPy*.

The Minimal Model

Pharmacokinetics is the study of how drugs and other substances move around the body, react, and are eliminated. In this chapter, I present a widely used pharmacokinetic model of glucose and insulin in the bloodstream.

Glucose is a form of sugar that circulates in the blood of animals; it is used as fuel for muscles, the brain, and other organs. The concentration of blood sugar is controlled by the hormone system, and especially by *insulin*, which is produced by the pancreas and has the effect of reducing blood sugar.

In people with normal pancreatic function, the hormone system maintains *homeostasis*; that is, it keeps the concentration of blood sugar in a range that is neither too high nor too low.

But if the pancreas does not produce enough insulin, or if the cells that should respond to insulin become insensitive, blood sugar can become elevated, a condition called *hyperglycemia*. Long-term, severe hyperglycemia is the defining symptom of *diabetes mellitus*, a serious disease that affects almost 10 percent of the US population.

A widely used test for hyperglycemia and diabetes is the frequently sampled intravenous glucose tolerance test (FSIGT), in which glucose is injected into the bloodstream of a fasting subject (someone who has not eaten recently); then blood samples are collected at intervals of 2–10 minutes for 3 hours. The samples are analyzed to measure the concentrations of glucose and insulin.

Using these measurements, we can estimate several parameters of the subject's response; the most important is a parameter denoted S_I, which quantifies the effect of insulin on the rate of reduction in blood sugar.

The Glucose Minimal Model

The minimal model, as proposed by Bergman, Ider, Bowden, and Cobelli in a 1979 paper, consists of two parts: the glucose model and the insulin model. I will present an implementation of the glucose model; you will have the chance to implement the insulin model as a case study.

The original model was developed in the 1970s; since then, many variations and extensions have been proposed. In his 2005 paper, Bergman comments on the development of the model, providing insight into their process:

> We applied the principle of Occam's razor, i.e. by asking what was the simplest model based upon known physiology that could account for the insulin–glucose relationship revealed in the data. Such a model must be simple enough to account totally for the measured glucose (given the insulin input), yet it must be possible, using mathematical techniques, to estimate all the characteristic parameters of the model from a single data set (thus avoiding unverifiable assumptions).

The most useful models are the ones that achieve this balance: including enough realism to capture the essential features of the system without so much complexity that they are impractical. In this example, the practical limit is the ability to estimate the parameters of the model using data, and to interpret the parameters meaningfully.

Bergman also discusses the features he and his colleagues thought were essential:

1. Glucose, once elevated by injection, returns to basal level due to two effects: the effect of glucose itself to normalize its own concentration [...] as well as the catalytic effect of insulin to allow glucose to self-normalize.

2. Also, we discovered that the effect of insulin on net glucose disappearance must be sluggish—that is, that insulin acts slowly because insulin must first move from plasma to a remote compartment [...] to exert its action on glucose disposal.

To paraphrase the second point, the effect of insulin on glucose disposal, as seen in the data, happens more slowly than we would expect if it depended primarily on the concentration of insulin in the blood. Bergman's group hypothesized that insulin must move relatively slowly from the blood to a remote compartment where it has its effect.

At the time, the "remote compartment" was a modeling abstraction that might, or might not, represent something physical. Later, according to Bergman, it was "shown to be interstitial fluid," that is, the fluid that surrounds tissue cells.

In the history of mathematical modeling, it is common for hypothetical entities, added to models to achieve particular effects, to be found later to correspond to physical entities. One notable example is the gene, which was defined as an inheritable unit several decades before we learned that genes are encoded in DNA (*https://en.wikipedia.org/wiki/Gene#Discovery_of_discrete_inherited_units*).

The glucose model consists of two differential equations:

$$\frac{dG}{dt} = -k_1 \left[G(t) - G_b \right] - X(t) G(t)$$

$$\frac{dX}{dt} = k_3 \left[I(t) - I_b \right] - k_2 X(t)$$

where

- G is the concentration of blood glucose as a function of time t, and dG/dt is its rate of change;

- X is the concentration of insulin in the tissue fluid as a function of time, and dX/dt is its rate of change;

- I is the concentration of insulin in the blood as a function of time, which is taken as an input into the model, based on measurements;

- G_b is the basal concentration of blood glucose, and I_b is the basal concentration of blood insulin, that is, the concentrations at equilibrium—both are constants estimated from measurements at the beginning or end of the test; and

- k_1, k_2, and k_3 are positive-valued parameters that control the rates of appearance and disappearance for glucose and insulin.

We can interpret the terms in the equations one by one:

- $-k_1 \left[G(t) - G_b \right]$ is the rate of glucose disappearance due to the effect of glucose itself. When $G(t)$ is above basal level, G_b, this term is negative; when $G(t)$ is below basal level, this term is positive. So in the absence of insulin, this term tends to restore blood glucose to basal level.

- $-X(t) G(t)$ models the interaction of glucose and insulin in tissue fluid, so the rate increases as either X or G increases. This term does not require a rate parameter because the units of X are unspecified; we can consider X to be in whatever units make the parameter of this term 1.

- $k_3 \left[I(t) - I_b \right]$ is the rate at which insulin diffuses between blood and tissue fluid. When $I(t)$ is above basal level, insulin diffuses from the blood into the tissue fluid. When $I(t)$ is below basal level, insulin diffuses from tissue to blood.

- $-k_2 X(t)$ is the rate of insulin disappearance in tissue fluid as it is consumed or broken down.

The initial state of the model is $X(0) = I_b$ and $G(0) = G_0$, where G_0 is a constant that represents the concentration of blood sugar immediately after the injection. In theory we could estimate G_0 based on measurements, but in practice it takes time for the injected glucose to spread through the blood volume. Since G_0 is not measurable, it is treated as a *free parameter* of the model, which means that we are free to choose it to fit the data.

Getting the Data

To develop and test the model, we'll use data from Pacini and Bergman's paper "MINMOD: A Computer Program to Calculate Insulin Sensitivity and Pancreatic Responsivity from the Frequently Sampled Intravenous Glucose Tolerance Test," published in *Computer Methods and Programs in Biomedicine* in 1986.

We can use pandas to read the data file:

```
from pandas import read_csv

data = read_csv('glucose_insulin.csv', index_col='time')
```

Here are the first few rows:

```
data.head()
```

time	glucose	insulin
0	92	11
2	350	26
4	287	130
6	251	85
8	240	51

data has two columns: glucose is the concentration of blood glucose in mg/dL; insulin is the concentration of insulin in the blood in µU/mL (a medical "unit," denoted U, is an amount defined by convention in context). The index is time in minutes.

This dataset represents glucose and insulin concentrations over 182 minutes for a subject with normal insulin production and sensitivity.

Interpolation

Before we are ready to implement the model, there's one problem we have to solve. In the differential equations, I is a function that can be evaluated at any time t. But in the DataFrame, we have measurements only at discrete times. The solution is *interpolation*, which estimates the value of I for values of t between the measurements.

To interpolate the values in I, we can use interpolate, which takes a Series as a parameter and returns a function. That's right, I said it returns a *function*. We can call interpolate like this:

```
I = interpolate(data.insulin)
```

The result is a function we can call like this:

```
I(18)
```

```
array(31.66666667)
```

In this example the interpolated value is about 31.7, which is a linear interpolation between the actual measurements at t = 16 and t = 19.

We can also pass an array as an argument to I. Here's an array of equally spaced values from t_0 to t_end:

```
t_0 = data.index[0]
t_end = data.index[-1]
t_array = linrange(t_0, t_end)
```

and here are the corresponding values of I:

```
I_array = I(t_array)
```

We can use `make_series` to put the results in a pandas Series:

```
I_series = make_series(t_array, I_array)
```

Here's what the interpolated values look like along with the data:

```
data.insulin.plot(style='o', color='C2', label='insulin data')
I_series.plot(color='C2', label='interpolation')

decorate(xlabel='Time (min)',
         ylabel='Concentration ($\mu$U/mL)')
```

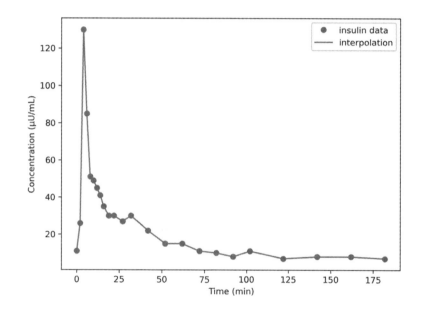

Linear interpolation connects the dots with straight lines, and for this dataset that's probably good enough. In the exercises at the end of the chapter, you can try out other kinds of interpolation.

Summary

This chapter introduced a model of the interaction between glucose and insulin in the bloodstream. It also introduced a new tool, interpolation, which we'll need to implement the model.

In the next chapter, we will use measured concentrations of insulin to simulate the glucose–insulin system, and we will compare the results to measured concentrations of glucose.

Then you'll have a chance to implement the second part of the model, which uses measured concentrations of glucose to simulate the insulin response, and compare the results to the data.

Exercises

17.1

interpolate is a wrapper for the SciPy function interp1d. Read the documentation of interp1d at *https://docs.scipy.org/doc/scipy/reference/generated/ scipy.interpolate.interp1d.html*.

In particular, notice the kind argument, which specifies a kind of interpolation. The default is linear interpolation, which connects the data points with straight lines.

Pass an argument to interpolate to specify one of the other kinds of interpolation and plot the results. Here's the plotting code again:

```
data.insulin.plot(style='o', color='C2', label='insulin data')
I_series.plot(color='C2', label='interpolation')

decorate(xlabel='Time (min)',
         ylabel='Concentration ($\mu$U/mL)')
```

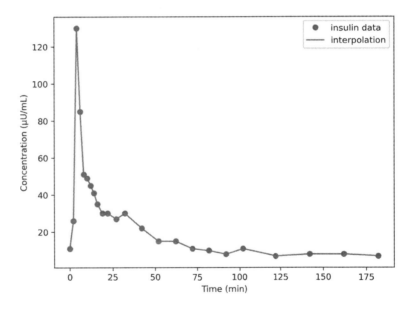

17.2

Interpolate the glucose data and generate a plot, similar to the previous one, that shows the data points and the interpolated curve evaluated at the time values in t_array.

18

IMPLEMENTING THE MINIMAL MODEL

The previous chapter presented the minimal model of the glucose–insulin system and introduced a tool we need to implement it: interpolation.

In this chapter, we'll implement the model in two ways:

- We'll start by rewriting the differential equations as difference equations; then we'll solve the difference equations using a version of run_simulation similar to what we have used in previous chapters.

- Then we'll use a new SciPy function, called solve_ivp, to solve the differential equation using a better algorithm.

We'll see that solve_ivp is faster and more accurate than run_simulation. As a result, we will use it for the models in the rest of the book.

This chapter is available as a Jupyter notebook where you can read the text, run the code, and work on the exercise. You can access the notebooks at *https://allendowney.github.io/ModSimPy*.

Implementing the Model

To get started, let's assume that the parameters of the model are known. We'll implement the model and use it to generate time series for G and X. Then we'll see how we can choose parameters that make the simulation fit the data.

Here are the parameters:

```
G0 = 270
k1 = 0.02
k2 = 0.02
k3 = 1.5e-05
```

We'll put these values in a sequence that we'll pass to make_system:

```
params = G0, k1, k2, k3
```

Here's a version of make_system that takes params and data as parameters:

```
def make_system(params, data):
    G0, k1, k2, k3 = params

    t_0 = data.index[0]
    t_end = data.index[-1]

    Gb = data.glucose[t_0]
    Ib = data.insulin[t_0]
    I = interpolate(data.insulin)

    init = State(G=G0, X=0)

    return System(init=init, params=params,
                  Gb=Gb, Ib=Ib, I=I,
                  t_0=t_0, t_end=t_end, dt=2)
```

make_system gets t_0 and t_end from the data. It uses the measurements at t = 0 as the basal levels, Gb and Ib. It uses the parameter G0 as the initial value for G. Then it packs everything into a System object:

```
system = make_system(params, data)
```

Now let's write the update function.

The Update Function

The minimal model is expressed in terms of differential equations:

$$\frac{dG}{dt} = -k_1 \left[G(t) - G_b \right] - X(t)\,G(t)$$

$$\frac{dX}{dt} = k_3 \left[I(t) - I_b \right] - k_2 X(t)$$

To simulate this system, we will rewrite them as difference equations. If we multiply both sides by dt, we have:

$$dG = \left[-k_1\left[G(t) - G_b\right] - X(t)\,G(t)\right]dt$$

$$dX = \left[k_3\left[I(t) - I_b\right] - k_2\,X(t)\right]dt$$

If we think of dt as a small step in time, these equations tell us how to compute the corresponding changes in G and X. Here's an update function that computes these changes:

```
def update_func(t, state, system):
    G, X = state
    G0, k1, k2, k3 = system.params
    I, Ib, Gb = system.I, system.Ib, system.Gb
    dt = system.dt

    dGdt = -k1 * (G - Gb) - X*G
    dXdt = k3 * (I(t) - Ib) - k2 * X

    G += dGdt * dt
    X += dXdt * dt

    return State(G=G, X=X)
```

As usual, the update function takes a timestamp, a State object, and a System object as parameters. The first line uses multiple assignment to extract the current values of G and X. The following lines unpack the parameters we need from the System object.

To compute the derivatives dGdt and dXdt we translate the equations from math notation to Python. Then, to perform the update, we multiply each derivative by the time step dt, which is two minutes in this example.

The return value is a State object with the new values of G and X.

Before running the simulation, it is a good idea to run the update function with the initial conditions:

```
update_func(system.t_0, system.init, system)
```

- -

	state
G	262.88
X	0.00

If it runs without errors and there is nothing obviously wrong with the results, we are ready to run the simulation.

Running the Simulation

We'll use the following version of `run_simulation`:

```python
def run_simulation(system, update_func):
    t_array = linrange(system.t_0, system.t_end, system.dt)
    n = len(t_array)

    frame = TimeFrame(index=t_array,
                      columns=system.init.index)
    frame.iloc[0] = system.init

    for i in range(n-1):
        t = t_array[i]
        state = frame.iloc[i]
        frame.iloc[i+1] = update_func(t, state, system)

    return frame
```

This version is similar to the one we used for the coffee cooling problem. The biggest difference is that it makes and returns a `TimeFrame`, which contains one column for each state variable, rather than a `TimeSeries`, which can only store one state variable.

When we make the `TimeFrame`, we use `index` to indicate that the index is the array of timestamps, `t_array`, and `columns` to indicate that the column names are the state variables we get from `init`.

We can run it like this:

```python
results = run_simulation(system, update_func)
```

The result is a `TimeFrame` with a row for each time step and a column for each of the state variables, `G` and `X`.

Here are the first few time steps:

```python
results.head()
```

	G	X
0.0	270.000000	0.000000
2.0	262.880000	0.000000
4.0	256.044800	0.000450
6.0	249.252568	0.004002
8.0	240.967447	0.006062

The following plot shows the simulated glucose levels from the model along with the measured data:

```
data.glucose.plot(style='o', alpha=0.5, label='glucose data')
results.G.plot(style='-', color='C0', label='simulation')

decorate(xlabel='Time (min)',
         ylabel='Concentration (mg/dL)')
```

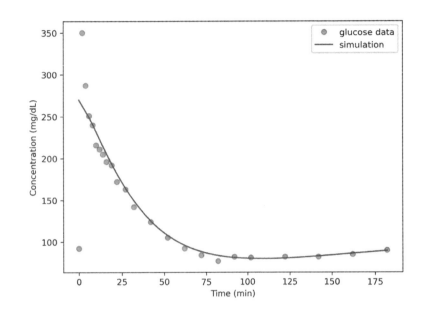

With the parameters we chose, the model fits the data well except during the first few minutes after the injection. But we don't expect the model to do well in this part of the time series.

The problem is that the model is *nonspatial*; that is, it does not take into account different concentrations in different parts of the body. Instead, it assumes that the concentrations of glucose and insulin in blood, and insulin in tissue fluid, are the same throughout the body. This way of representing the body is known among experts as the "bag of blood" model.

Immediately after injection, it takes time for the injected glucose to circulate. During that time, we don't expect a nonspatial model to be accurate. For this reason, we should not take the estimated value of G0 too seriously; it is useful for fitting the model, but not meant to correspond to a physical, measurable quantity.

The following plot shows simulated insulin levels in the hypothetical remote compartment, which is in unspecified units:

```
results.X.plot(color='C1', label='remote insulin')

decorate(xlabel='Time (min)',
         ylabel='Concentration (arbitrary units)')
```

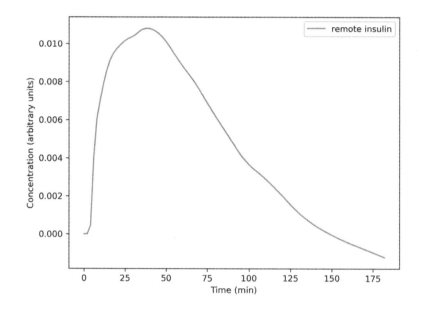

Remember that X represents the concentration of insulin in the remote compartment, which is believed to be tissue fluid, so we can't compare it to the measured concentration of insulin in the blood.

X rises quickly after the initial injection and then declines as the concentration of glucose declines. Qualitatively, this behavior is as expected, but because X is not an observable quantity, we can't validate this part of the model quantitatively.

Solving Differential Equations

To implement the minimal model, we rewrote the differential equations as difference equations with a finite time step, dt. When dt is very small, or more precisely *infinitesimal*, the difference equations are the same as the differential equations. But in our simulations, dt is two minutes, which is not very small, and definitely not infinitesimal.

In effect, the simulations assume that the derivatives dG/dt and dX/dt are constant during each two-minute time step. This method, evaluating derivatives at discrete time steps and assuming that they are constant in between, is called *Euler's method*.

Euler's method is good enough for many problems, but sometimes it is not very accurate. In that case, we can usually make it more accurate by decreasing the size of *dt*. But then it is not very efficient.

There are other methods that are more accurate and more efficient than Euler's method. SciPy provides several of them wrapped in a function called solve_ivp. The ivp stands for *initial value problem*, which is the term for problems like the ones we've been solving, where we are given the initial conditions and try to predict what will happen.

The ModSim library provides a function called run_solve_ivp that makes solve_ivp a little easier to use. To use it, we have to provide a *slope function*, which is similar to an update function; in fact, it takes the same parameters: a timestamp, a State object, and a System object. Here's a slope function that evaluates the differential equations of the minimal model:

```
def slope_func(t, state, system):
    G, X = state
    G0, k1, k2, k3 = system.params
    I, Ib, Gb = system.I, system.Ib, system.Gb

    dGdt = -k1 * (G - Gb) - X*G
    dXdt = k3 * (I(t) - Ib) - k2 * X

    return dGdt, dXdt
```

slope_func is a little simpler than update_func because it computes only the derivatives, that is, the slopes. It doesn't do the updates; the solver does them for us.

Now we can call run_solve_ivp like this:

```
results2, details = run_solve_ivp(system, slope_func,
                         t_eval=results.index)
```

run_solve_ivp is similar to run_simulation: it takes a System object and a slope function as parameters. The third argument, t_eval, is optional; it specifies where the solution should be evaluated.

It returns two values: a TimeFrame, which we assign to results2, and an OdeResult object, which we assign to details.

The OdeResult object contains information about how the solver ran, including a success code:

```
details.success
```

```
True
```

and a diagnostic message:

```
details.message
```

```
'The solver successfully reached the end of the integration interval.'
```

It's important to check these messages after running the solver, in case anything went wrong.

The TimeFrame has one row for each time step and one column for each state variable. In this example, the rows are the time steps from 0 to 182 minutes; the columns are the state variables, G and X. Here are the first few time steps:

```
results2.head()
```

	G	X
0.0	270.000000	0.000000
2.0	262.980942	0.000240
4.0	255.683455	0.002525
6.0	247.315442	0.005174
8.0	238.271851	0.006602

Because we used t_eval=results.index, the timestamps in results2 are the same as in results, which makes them easier to compare.

The following figure shows the results from run_solve_ivp along with the results from run_simulation:

```
results.G.plot(style='--', label='simulation')
results2.G.plot(style='-', label='solve ivp')

decorate(xlabel='Time (min)',
         ylabel='Concentration (mg/dL)')
```

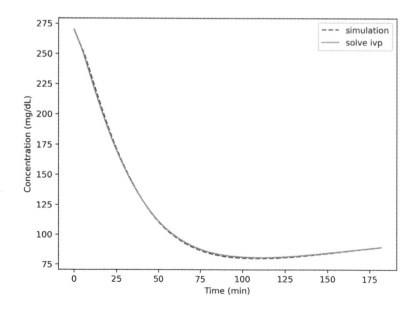

The differences are barely visible. We can compute the relative differences like this:

```
diff = results.G - results2.G
percent_diff = diff / results2.G * 100
```

and we can use describe to compute summary statistics:

```
percent_diff.abs().describe()
```

	G
count	92.000000
mean	0.649121
std	0.392903
min	0.000000
25%	0.274854
50%	0.684262
75%	1.009868
max	1.278168

The mean relative difference is about 0.65 percent, and the maximum is a little more than 1 percent.

Here are the results for X:

```
results.X.plot(style='--', label='simulation')
results2.X.plot(style='-', label='solve ivp')

decorate(xlabel='Time (min)',
         ylabel='Concentration (arbitrary units)')
```

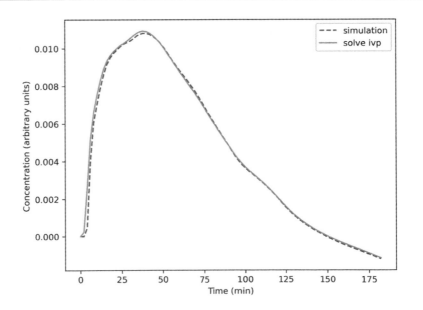

These differences are a little bigger, especially at the beginning.

If we use `run_simulation` with smaller time steps, the results are more accurate, but they take longer to compute. For some problems, we can find a value of `dt` that produces accurate results in a reasonable time. However, if `dt` is *too* small, the results can be inaccurate again. So it can be tricky to get it right.

The advantage of `run_solve_ivp` is that it chooses the time step automatically in order to balance accuracy and efficiency. You can use arguments to adjust this balance, but most of the time the results are accurate enough, and the computation is fast enough, without any intervention.

Summary

In this chapter, we implemented the glucose minimal model two ways, using `run_simulation` and `run_solve_ivp`, and compared the results. We found that in this example, `run_simulation`, which uses Euler's method, is probably good enough. But soon we will see examples where it is not.

So far, we have assumed that the parameters of the system are known, but in practice that's not true. As one of the case studies in the next chapter, you'll have a chance to see where those parameters came from.

Exercise

18.1

Our solution to the differential equations is approximate because we used a finite step size, `dt=2` minutes. If we make the step size smaller, we expect the solution to be more accurate. Run the simulation with `dt=1` and compare the results. What is the largest relative error between the two solutions?

19

CASE STUDIES PART II

This chapter presents case studies where you can apply the tools we have learned so far to the glucose-insulin minimal model, an electronic circuit, a thermal model of a wall, and the interaction of HIV and T cells.

This chapter is available as a Jupyter notebook where you can read the text, run the code, and work on the case studies. You can access the notebooks at *https://allendowney.github.io/ModSimPy*.

Revisiting the Minimal Model

In the previous chapter we implemented the glucose minimal model using given parameters, but I didn't say where those parameters came from.

In the repository for this book, you will find a notebook, *glucose.ipynb*, that shows how we can find the parameters that best fit the data. You can download it from *https://github.com/AllenDowney/ModSimPy/raw/master/examples/glucose.ipynb* or run it on Colab at *https://colab.research.google.com/github/AllenDowney/ModSimPy/blob/master/examples/glucose.ipynb*.

It uses a SciPy function called leastsq, which stands for "least squares," so named because it finds the parameters that minimize the sum of squared differences between the results of the model and the data.

You can think of `leastsq` as an optional tool for this book. We won't use it in the text itself, but it appears in a few of the case studies.

The Insulin Minimal Model

Along with the glucose minimal model, Bergman and Pacini developed an insulin minimal model, in which the concentration of insulin, I, is governed by this differential equation:

$$\frac{dI}{dt} = -kI(t) + \gamma \left[G(t) - G_T \right] t$$

where

- k is a parameter that controls the rate of insulin disappearance independent of blood glucose;

- $G(t)$ is the measured concentration of blood glucose at time t;

- G_T is the glucose threshold—when blood glucose is above this level, it triggers an increase in blood insulin; and

- γ is a parameter that controls the rate of increase (or decrease) in blood insulin when glucose is above (or below) G_T.

The initial condition is $I(0) = I_0$. As in the glucose minimal model, we treat this initial concentration as a free parameter; that is, we'll choose it to fit the data.

The parameters of this model can be used to estimate ϕ_1 and ϕ_2, which are quantities that, according to Bergman and Pacini, "describe the sensitivity to glucose of the first and second phase pancreatic responsivity." These quantities are related to the parameters as follows:

$$\phi_1 = \frac{I_{max} - I_b}{k(G_0 - G_b)}$$

$$\phi_2 = \gamma \times 10^4$$

where I_{max} is the maximum measured insulin level, and I_b and G_b are the basal levels of insulin and glucose.

In the repository for this book, you will find a notebook, *insulin.ipynb*, that contains starter code for this case study. Use it to implement the insulin model, find the parameters that best fit the data, and estimate ϕ_1 and ϕ_2. You can download it from *https://github.com/AllenDowney/ModSimPy/raw/ master/examples/insulin.ipynb* or run it on Colab at*https://colab.research.google .com/github/AllenDowney/ModSimPy/blob/master/examples/insulin.ipynb*.

Low-Pass Filter

The circuit diagram in Figure 19-1 shows a low-pass filter built with one resistor and one capacitor.

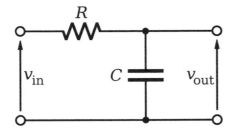

Figure 19-1: A circuit diagram of a low-pass RC filter

A *filter* is a circuit that takes a signal, V_{in}, as input and produces a signal, V_{out}, as output. In this context, a *signal* is a voltage that changes over time.

A filter is *low-pass* if it allows low-frequency signals to pass from V_{in} to V_{out} unchanged, but it reduces the amplitude of high-frequency signals.

By applying the laws of circuit analysis, we can derive a differential equation that describes the behavior of this system. By solving the differential equation, we can predict the effect of this circuit on any input signal.

Suppose we are given V_{in} and V_{out} at a particular instant in time. By Ohm's law, which is a simple model of the behavior of resistors, the instantaneous current through the resistor is:

$$I_R = (V_{in} - V_{out})/R$$

where R is resistance in ohms (Ω).

Assuming that no current flows through the output of the circuit, Kirchhoff's current law implies that the current through the capacitor is:

$$I_C = I_R$$

According to a simple model of the behavior of capacitors, current through the capacitor causes a change in the voltage across the capacitor:

$$I_C = C\frac{dV_{out}}{dt}$$

where C is capacitance in farads (F). Combining these equations yields a differential equation for V_{out}:

$$\frac{dV_{out}}{dt} = \frac{V_{in} - V_{out}}{RC}$$

In the repository for this book, you will find a notebook, *filter.ipynb*, which contains starter code for this case study. You can download it from *https://github.com/AllenDowney/ModSimPy/raw/master/examples/filter.ipynb* or run it on Colab at *https://colab.research.google.com/github/AllenDowney/ModSimPy/blob/master/examples/filter.ipynb*. Follow the instructions to simulate the low-pass filter for input signals like this:

$$V_{in}(t) = A\cos(2\pi ft)$$

where A is the amplitude of the input signal, say 5 V, and f is the frequency of the signal in hertz (Hz).

Thermal Behavior of a Wall

This case study is based on a paper by Gori et al. that models the thermal behavior of a brick wall with the goal of understanding the "performance gap between the expected energy use of buildings and their measured energy use."

Figure 19-2 shows the scenario and their model of the wall.

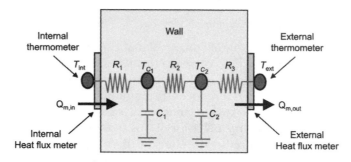

Figure 19-2: A model of the thermal behavior of a wall (from Gori et al., 2017)

On the interior and exterior surfaces of the wall, they measure temperature and heat flux (rate of heat flow) over a period of three days. They model the wall using two thermal masses connected to the surfaces, and to each other, by thermal resistors.

The primary methodology of the paper is a statistical method for inferring the parameters of the system (two thermal masses and three thermal resistances).

The primary result is a comparison of two models: the one shown here with two thermal masses, and a simpler model with only one thermal mass. They find that the two-mass model is able to reproduce the measured fluxes substantially better.

For this case study we will implement their model and run it with the estimated parameters from the paper, and then use leastsq to see if we can find parameters that yield lower errors.

In the repository for this book, you will find a notebook, *wall.ipynb*, with the code and results for this case study. You can download it from *https://github.com/AllenDowney/ModSimPy/raw/master/examples/wall.ipynb* or run it on Colab at *https://colab.research.google.com/github/AllenDowney/ModSimPy/blob/master/examples/wall.ipynb*.

The paper this case study is based on is by Gori, Marincioni, Biddulph, and Elwell: "Inferring the Thermal Resistance and Effective Thermal Mass Distribution of a Wall from In Situ Measurements to Characterise Heat Transfer at Both the Interior and Exterior Surfaces," published in *Energy and Buildings* in 2017 (available at *https://www.sciencedirect.com/science/article/pii/S0378778816313056*). The authors put their paper under a Creative Commons license and made their data available at *https://discovery.ucl.ac.uk/id/eprint/1526521*. I thank them for their commitment to open, reproducible science, which made this case study possible.

HIV

During the initial phase of HIV infection, the concentration of the virus in the bloodstream typically increases quickly and then decreases. The most obvious explanation for the decline is an immune response that destroys the virus or controls its replication. However, at least in some patients, the decline occurs even without any detectable immune response.

In 1996 Andrew Phillips proposed another explanation for the decline in this paper: "Reduction of HIV Concentration During Acute Infection: Independence from a Specific Immune Response," published in *Science* in January 1996 (see *https://pubmed.ncbi.nlm.nih.gov/8560262*).

Phillips presents a system of differential equations that models the concentrations of the HIV virus and the CD4 cells it infects. The model does not include an immune response; nevertheless, it demonstrates behavior that is qualitatively similar to what is seen in patients during the first few weeks after infection.

His conclusion is that the observed decline in the concentration of HIV might not be caused by an immune response; it could be due to the dynamic interaction between HIV and the cells it infects.

In the repository for this book, you will find a notebook, *hiv_model.ipynb*, which you can use to implement Phillips's model and consider whether it does the work it is meant to do. You can download it from *https://github .com/AllenDowney/ModSimPy/raw/master/examples/glucose.ipynb* or run it on Colab at *https://colab.research.google.com/github/AllenDowney/ModSimPy/blob/ master/examples/hiv_model.ipynb*.

PART III

SECOND-ORDER SYSTEMS

20

THE FALLING PENNY REVISITED

 So far the differential equations we've worked with have been *first-order*, which means they involve only first derivatives. In this chapter, we turn our attention to *second-order* differential equations, which can involve both first and second derivatives.

We will revisit the falling penny example from Chapter 1 and use run_solve_ivp to find the position and velocity of the penny as it falls, with and without air resistance.

This chapter is available as a Jupyter notebook where you can read the text, run the code, and work on the exercise. You can access the notebooks at *https://allendowney.github.io/ModSimPy*.

Newton's Second Law of Motion

First-order differential equations (DEs) can be written as:

$$\frac{dy}{dx} = G(x, y)$$

where G is some function of x and y.

Second-order DEs can be written as:

$$\frac{d^2 y}{dx^2} = H(x, y, \frac{dy}{dx})$$

where H is a function of x, y, and dy/dx.

In this chapter, we will work with one of the most famous and useful second-order DEs, Newton's second law of motion:

$$F = ma$$

where F is a force or the total of a set of forces, m is the mass of a moving object, and a is its acceleration.

Newton's law might not look like a differential equation, until we realize that acceleration, a, is the second derivative of position, y, with respect to time, t. With the substitution

$$a = \frac{d^2 y}{dt^2}$$

Newton's law can be written as:

$$\frac{d^2 y}{dt^2} = F/m$$

and that's definitely a second-order DE. In general, F can be a function of time, position, and velocity.

Of course, this "law" is really a model in the sense that it is a simplification of the real world. Although it is often approximately true, keep the following in mind:

- It only applies if m is constant; if mass depends on time, position, or velocity, we have to use a more general form of Newton's law (*https://en.wikipedia.org/wiki/Newton's_laws_of_motion*).

- It is not a good model for very small things, which are better described by another model, quantum mechanics.

- It is not a good model for things moving very fast, which are better described by yet another model, relativistic mechanics.

However, for medium-sized things with constant mass, moving at medium-sized speeds, Newton's model is extremely useful. If we can quantify the forces that act on such an object, we can predict how it will move.

Dropping Pennies

As a first example, let's get back to the penny falling from the Empire State Building, which we considered in Chapter 1. We will implement two models of this system: first without air resistance, then with.

Given that the Empire State Building is 381 m high, and assuming that the penny is dropped from a standstill, the initial conditions are:

```
init = State(y=381, v=0)
```

where y is height above the sidewalk and v is velocity.

Let's put the initial conditions in a System object, along with the magnitude of acceleration due to gravity, g, and the duration of the simulations, t_end:

```
system = System(init=init,
                g=9.8,
                t_end=10)
```

Now we need a slope function, and here's where things get tricky. As we have seen, run_solve_ivp can solve systems of first-order DEs, but Newton's law is a second-order DE. However, if we recognize that

1. velocity, v, is the derivative of position, dy/dt; and

2. acceleration, a, is the derivative of velocity, dv/dt,

we can rewrite Newton's law as a system of first-order DEs:

$$\frac{dy}{dt} = v$$

$$\frac{dv}{dt} = a$$

We can then translate those equations into a slope function:

```
def slope_func(t, state, system):
    y, v = state

    dydt = v
    dvdt = -system.g

    return dydt, dvdt
```

As usual, the parameters are a timestamp, a State object, and a System object.

The first line unpacks the state variables, y and v. The next two lines compute the derivatives of the state variables, dydt and dvdt. The derivative of position is velocity, and the derivative of velocity is acceleration. In this case, $a = -g$, which indicates that acceleration due to gravity is in the direction of decreasing y. slope_func returns a sequence containing the two derivatives.

Before calling run_solve_ivp, it is a good idea to test the slope function with the initial conditions:

```
dydt, dvdt = slope_func(0, system.init, system)
dydt, dvdt
```

```
(0, -9.8)
```

The result is 0 m/s for velocity and −9.8 m/s² for acceleration.

Now we call run_solve_ivp like this:

```
results, details = run_solve_ivp(system, slope_func)
details.message
```

'The solver successfully reached the end of the integration interval.'

results is a TimeFrame with two columns: y contains the height of the penny; v contains its velocity. Here are the first few rows:

```
results.head()
```

	y	v
0.0	381.000	0.00
0.1	380.951	−0.98
0.2	380.804	−1.96
0.3	380.559	−2.94
0.4	380.216	−3.92

We can plot the results like this:

```
results.y.plot()

decorate(xlabel='Time (s)',
         ylabel='Position (m)')
```

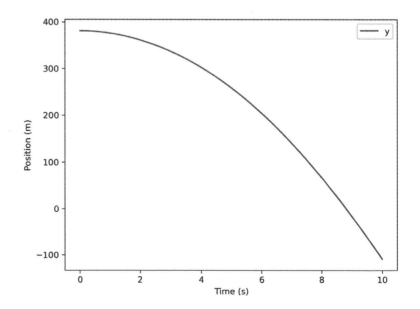

Since acceleration is constant, velocity increases linearly and position decreases quadratically; as a result, the height curve is a parabola.

The last value of results.y is negative:

```
results.iloc[-1].y
```

```
-108.99999999999983
```

This means we ran the simulation too long. One way to solve this problem is to use the results to estimate the time when the penny hits the sidewalk.

The ModSim library provides crossings, which takes a TimeSeries and a value, and returns a sequence of times when the series passes through the value. We can find the time when the height of the penny is 0 like this:

```
t_crossings = crossings(results.y, 0)
t_crossings
```

```
array([8.81788535])
```

The result is an array with a single value, 8.818 s. Now, we could run the simulation again with t_end = 8.818, but there's a better way.

Event Functions

As an option, run_solve_ivp can take an *event function*, which detects an "event," like the penny hitting the sidewalk, and ends the simulation.

Event functions take the same parameters as slope functions: t, state, and system. They should return a value that passes through 0 when the event occurs. Here's an event function that detects the penny hitting the sidewalk:

```
def event_func(t, state, system):
    y, v = state
    return y
```

The return value is the height of the penny, y, which passes through 0 when the penny hits the sidewalk.

We pass the event function to run_solve_ivp like this:

```
results, details = run_solve_ivp(system, slope_func,
                                 events=event_func)
details.message
```

```
'A termination event occurred.'
```

Then we can get the flight time like this:

```
t_end = results.index[-1]
t_end
```

```
8.817885349720553
```

and the final velocity like this:

```
y, v = results.iloc[-1]
y, v
```

```
(0.0, -86.41527642726145)
```

If there were no air resistance, the penny would hit the sidewalk (or someone's head) at about 86 m/s. So it's a good thing there is air resistance.

Summary

In this chapter, we wrote Newton's second law, which is a second-order DE, as a system of first-order DEs. Then we used run_solve_ivp to simulate a penny dropping from the Empire State Building in the absence of air resistance. And we used an event function to stop the simulation when the penny reaches the sidewalk.

In the next chapter, we'll add air resistance to the model.

Exercise

20.1

Here's a question from the website Ask an Astronomer (*http://curious .astro.cornell.edu/about-us/39-our-solar-system/the-earth/other-catastrophes/57 -how-long-would-it-take-the-earth-to-fall-into-the-sun-intermediate*): "If the Earth suddenly stopped orbiting the Sun, I know eventually it would be pulled in by the Sun's gravity and hit it. How long would it take the Earth to hit the Sun? I imagine it would go slowly at first and then pick up speed." Use run_solve_ivp to answer this question.

Here are some suggestions about how to proceed:

1. Look up the law of universal gravitation and any constants you need. I suggest you work entirely in SI units: meters, kilograms, and newtons.
2. When the distance between the Earth and the Sun gets small, this system behaves badly, so you should use an event function to stop when the surface of Earth reaches the surface of the Sun.
3. Express your answer in days, and plot the results as millions of kilometers versus days.

If you read the reply by Dave Rothstein, you will see other ways to solve the problem, and a good discussion of the modeling decisions behind them.

You might also be interested to know that it's not that easy to get to the Sun; see *https://www.theatlantic.com/science/archive/2018/08/ parker-solar-probe-launch-nasa/567197*.

21

DRAG

In the previous chapter, we simulated a penny falling in a vacuum, that is, without air resistance. But the computational framework we used is very general; it is easy to add additional forces, including drag. In this chapter, I'll present a model of drag force and add it to the simulation.

This chapter is available as a Jupyter notebook where you can read the text, run the code, and work on the exercises. You can access the notebooks at *https://allendowney.github.io/ModSimPy*.

Calculating Drag Force

As an object moves through a fluid, like air, the object applies force to the air and, in accordance with Newton's third law of motion, the air applies an equal and opposite force to the object. The direction of this *drag force* is opposite the direction of travel, and its magnitude is given by the drag equation (*https://en.wikipedia.org/wiki/Drag_equation*):

$$F_d = \frac{1}{2}\rho \, v^2 \, C_d \, A$$

where

- F_d is force due to drag, in newtons (N), which are the SI units of force (1 N = 1 kg m/s^2);

- ρ is the density of the fluid in kg/m^3;

- v is the magnitude of velocity in m/s;

- A is the *reference area* of the object in m^2. In this context, the reference area is the projected frontal area, that is, the visible area of the object as seen from a point on its line of travel (and far away); and

- C_d is the *drag coefficient*, a dimensionless quantity that depends on the shape of the object (including length but not frontal area), its surface properties, and how it interacts with the fluid.

For objects moving at moderate speeds through air, typical drag coefficients are between 0.1 and 1.0, with blunt objects at the high end of the range and streamlined objects at the low end. For simple geometric objects we can sometimes guess the drag coefficient with reasonable accuracy; for more complex objects we usually have to take measurements and estimate C_d from data.

Of course, the drag equation is itself a model, based on the assumption that C_d does not depend on the other terms in the equation: density, velocity, and area. For objects moving in air at moderate speeds (below 45 miles per hour or 20 m/s), this model might be good enough, but we will revisit this assumption in the next chapter.

For the falling penny, we can use measurements to estimate C_d. In particular, we can measure *terminal velocity*, v_{term}, which is the speed where drag force equals force due to gravity:

$$\frac{1}{2} \, \rho \, v_{term}^2 \, C_d \, A = mg$$

where m is the mass of the object and g is acceleration due to gravity. Solving this equation for C_d yields:

$$C_d = \frac{2 \, mg}{\rho \, v_{term}^2 \, A}$$

According to *MythBusters*, the terminal velocity of a penny is between 35 and 65 miles per hour. Using the low end of their range, 40 miles per hour, or about 18 m/s, the estimated value of C_d is 0.44, which is close to the drag coefficient of a smooth sphere.

Now we are ready to add air resistance to the model. But first I want to introduce one more computational tool, the Params object.

The Params Object

As the number of system parameters increases, and as we need to do more work to compute them, we will find it useful to define a `Params` object to contain the quantities we need to make a `System` object. `Params` objects are similar to `System` objects, and we initialize them the same way.

Here's the `Params` object for the falling penny:

```
params = Params(
    mass=0.0025, # kg
    diameter=0.019, # m
    rho=1.2, # kg/m**3
    g=9.8, # m/s**2
    v_init=0, # m / s
    v_term=18, # m / s
    height=381, # m
    t_end=30, # s
)
```

The mass and diameter are from *https://en.wikipedia.org/wiki/Penny_(United _States_coin)*. The density of air depends on temperature, barometric pressure (which depends on altitude), humidity, and composition. I chose a value that might be typical in New York City at 20°C.

Here's a version of `make_system` that takes a `Params` object and makes a `System` object:

```
from numpy import pi

def make_system(params):
    init = State(y=params.height, v=params.v_init)

    area = pi * (params.diameter / 2)**2

    C_d = (2 * params.mass * params.g /
           (params.rho * area * params.v_term**2))

    return System(init=init,
                  area=area,
                  C_d=C_d,
                  mass=params.mass,
                  rho=params.rho,
                  g=params.g,
                  t_end=params.t_end)
```

The `System` object contains the parameters we need for the simulation, including the initial state, the area of the penny, and the coefficient of drag.

Here's how we call this function:

```
system = make_system(params)
```

Based on the mass and diameter of the penny, the density of air, the acceleration due to gravity, and the observed terminal velocity, we estimate that the coefficient of drag is about 0.44:

```
system.C_d
```

```
0.4445009981135434
```

It might not be obvious why it is useful to create a Params object just to create a System object. In fact, if we run only one simulation, it might not be useful. But it helps when we want to change or sweep the parameters.

For example, suppose we learn that the terminal velocity of a penny is actually closer to 20 m/s. We can make a Params object with the new value, and a corresponding System object, like this:

```
params2 = params.set(v_term=20)
```

The result from set is a new Params object that is identical to the original except for the given value of v_term. If we pass params2 to make_system, we see that it computes a different value of C_d:

```
system2 = make_system(params2)
system2.C_d
```

```
0.3600458084719701
```

If the terminal velocity of the penny is 20 m/s, rather than 18 m/s, that implies that the coefficient of drag is 0.36, rather than 0.44. And that makes sense, since lower drag implies faster terminal velocity.

Using Params objects to make System objects helps make sure that relationships like this are consistent.

Simulating the Penny Drop

Now let's get to the simulation. Here's a version of the slope function that includes drag:

```
def slope_func(t, state, system):
    y, v = state
    rho, C_d, area = system.rho, system.C_d, system.area
    mass, g = system.mass, system.g

    f_drag = rho * v**2 * C_d * area / 2
    a_drag = f_drag / mass

    dydt = v
    dvdt = -g + a_drag

    return dydt, dvdt
```

As usual, the parameters of the slope function are a timestamp, a State object, and a System object. We don't use t in this example, but we can't leave it out because when run_solve_ivp calls the slope function, it always provides the same arguments, whether they are needed or not.

f_drag is force due to drag, based on the drag equation. a_drag is acceleration due to drag, based on Newton's second law.

To compute total acceleration, we add accelerations due to gravity and drag. g is negated because it is in the direction of decreasing y; a_drag is positive because it is in the direction of increasing y. In the next chapter, we will use Vector objects to keep track of the direction of forces and add them up in a less error-prone way.

As usual, let's test the slope function with the initial conditions:

```
slope_func(0, system.init, system)
```

```
(0, -9.8)
```

Because the initial velocity is 0, so is the drag force, so the initial acceleration is still g.

To stop the simulation when the penny hits the sidewalk, we'll use the event function from the previous chapter:

```
def event_func(t, state, system):
    y, v = state
    return y
```

Now we can run the simulation like this:

```
results, details = run_solve_ivp(system, slope_func,
                                 events=event_func)
details.message
```

```
'A termination event occurred.'
```

Here are the last few time steps:

```
results.tail()
```

	y	v
21.541886	1.614743e+01	−18.001510
21.766281	1.211265e+01	−18.006240
21.990676	8.076745e+00	−18.009752
22.215070	4.039275e+00	−18.011553
22.439465	2.131628e-14	−18.011383

The final height is close to 0, as expected. Interestingly, the final velocity is not exactly terminal velocity, which is a reminder that the simulation results are only approximate.

We can get the flight time from results:

```
t_sidewalk = results.index[-1]
t_sidewalk
```

```
22.439465058044306
```

With air resistance, it takes about 22 seconds for the penny to reach the sidewalk.

Here's a plot of position as a function of time:

```
def plot_position(results):
    results.y.plot()

    decorate(xlabel='Time (s)',
        ylabel='Position (m)')

plot_position(results)
```

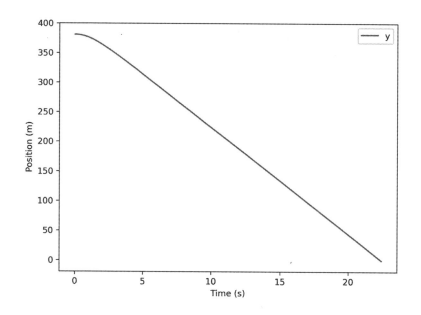

And here's a plot of velocity as a function of time:

```
def plot_velocity(results):

    results.v.plot(color='C1', label='v')

    decorate(xlabel='Time (s)',
            ylabel='Velocity (m/s)')

plot_velocity(results)
```

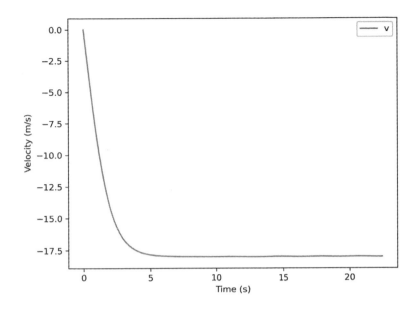

From an initial velocity of 0, the penny accelerates downward until it reaches terminal velocity; after that, velocity is constant.

Summary

This chapter presents a model of drag force, which we use to estimate the coefficient of drag for a penny, and then simulate, one more time, dropping a penny from the Empire State Building.

In the next chapter we'll move from one dimension to two, simulating the flight of a baseball.

Exercises

21.1

Run the simulation with a downward initial velocity that exceeds the penny's terminal velocity.

What do you expect to happen? Plot velocity and position as a function of time, and see if they are consistent with your prediction.

Hint: Use params.set to make a new Params object with a different initial velocity.

21.2

Suppose we drop a quarter from the Empire State Building and find that its flight time is 19.1 seconds. Use this measurement to estimate terminal velocity and coefficient of drag.

You can get the relevant dimensions of a quarter from *https://en .wikipedia.org/wiki/Quarter_(United_States_coin)*.

1. Create a `Params` object with new values of `mass` and `diameter`. We don't know `v_term`, so we'll start with the initial guess 18 m/s.
2. Use `make_system` to create a `System` object.
3. Call `run_solve_ivp` to simulate the system. How does the flight time of the simulation compare to the measurement?
4. Try a few different values of `v_term` and see if you can get the simulated flight time close to 19.1 seconds.
5. Optionally, write an error function and use `root_scalar` to improve your estimate.
6. Use your best estimate of `v_term` to compute `C_d`.

Note: I fabricated the "observed" flight time, so don't take the results of this exercise too seriously.

22

TWO-DIMENSIONAL MOTION

In the previous chapter, we modeled an object moving in one dimension, with and without drag. Now let's move on to two dimensions, and baseball!

In this chapter we'll model the flight of a baseball including the effect of air resistance. In the next chapter we'll use this model to solve an optimization problem.

This chapter is available as a Jupyter notebook where you can read the text, run the code, and work on the exercises. You can access the notebooks at *https://allendowney.github.io/ModSimPy*.

Assumptions and Decisions

To model the flight of a baseball, we have to make some decisions. To get started, we'll ignore any spin that might be on the ball, and the resulting Magnus force. Under this assumption, the ball travels in a vertical plane, so we'll run simulations in two dimensions, rather than three.

To model air resistance, we'll need the mass, frontal area, and drag coefficient of a baseball. Mass and diameter are easy to find (*https://en.wikipedia.org/wiki/Baseball_(ball)*). Drag coefficient is only a little harder; according to R.K. Adair's *The Physics of Baseball* (Harper & Row, 1990), the drag coefficient of a baseball is approximately 0.33 (with no units).

However, this value *does* depend on velocity. At low velocities it might be as high as 0.5, and at high velocities as low as 0.28. Furthermore, the transition between these values typically happens exactly in the range of velocities we are interested in, between 20 m/s and 40 m/s.

Nevertheless, we'll start with a simple model where the drag coefficient does not depend on velocity; as an exercise at the end of the chapter, you can implement a more detailed model and see what effect it has on the results.

But first we need a new computational tool, the Vector object.

Vectors

Now that we are working in two dimensions, it will be useful to work with *vector quantities*, that is, quantities that represent both a magnitude and a direction. We will use vectors to represent positions, velocities, accelerations, and forces in two and three dimensions.

ModSim provides a function called Vector that creates a pandas Series that contains the *components* of the vector. In a Vector that represents a position in space, the components are the x- and y-coordinates in two dimensions, plus a z-coordinate if the Vector is in three dimensions.

You can create a Vector by specifying its components. The following Vector represents a point three units to the right (or east) and four units up (or north) from an implicit origin:

```
A = Vector(3, 4)
show(A)
```

	component
x	3
y	4

You can access the components of a Vector by name using the dot operator, like this:

```
A.x
```

```
3
```

or this:

```
A.y
```

```
4
```

You can also access them by index using square brackets, like this:

```
A[0]
```

```
3
```

or this:

```
A[1]
```

```
4
```

Vector objects support most mathematical operations, including addition:

```
B = Vector(1, 2)
show(A + B)
```

	component
x	4
y	6

and subtraction:

```
show(A - B)
```

	component
x	2
y	2

For the definition and graphical interpretation of these operations, see *https://en.wikipedia.org/wiki/Euclidean_vector#Addition_and_subtraction*.

We can specify a Vector with coordinates x and y, as in the previous examples. Equivalently, we can specify a Vector with a magnitude and angle.

Magnitude is the length of the vector: if the Vector represents a position, magnitude is its distance from the origin; if it represents a velocity, magnitude is its speed.

The *angle* of a Vector is its direction, expressed as an angle in radians from the positive x-axis. In the Cartesian plane, the angle 0 rad is due east, and the angle π rad is due west.

ModSim provides functions to compute the magnitude and angle of a Vector. For example, here are the magnitude and angle of A:

```
mag = vector_mag(A)
theta = vector_angle(A)
mag, theta
```

```
(5.0, 0.9272952180016122)
```

The magnitude is 5 because the length of A is the hypotenuse of a 3-4-5 triangle.

The result from vector_angle is in radians. Most Python functions, like sin and cos, work with radians, but many people find it more natural to work with degrees. Fortunately, NumPy provides a function to convert radians to degrees:

```
from numpy import rad2deg

angle = rad2deg(theta)
angle
```

```
53.13010235415598
```

and a function to convert degrees to radians:

```
from numpy import deg2rad

theta = deg2rad(angle)
theta
```

```
0.9272952180016122
```

To avoid confusion, we'll use the variable name angle for a value in degrees and theta for a value in radians.

If you are given an angle and magnitude, you can make a Vector using pol2cart, which converts from polar to Cartesian coordinates. For example, here's a new Vector with the same angle and magnitude of A:

```
x, y = pol2cart(theta, mag)
C = Vector(x, y)
show(C)
```
---

	component
x	3.0
y	4.0

Another way to represent the direction of A is a *unit vector*, which is a vector with magnitude 1 that points in the same direction as A. You can compute a unit vector by dividing a vector by its magnitude:

```
show(A / vector_mag(A))
```

---

	component
x	0.6
y	0.8

ModSim provides a function that does the same thing, called vector_hat because unit vectors are conventionally decorated with a hat, like this: $\widehat{A}$. Here's how to use it:

```
A_hat = vector_hat(A)
show(A_hat)
```

---

	component
x	0.6
y	0.8

Now let's get back to the game.

Simulating Baseball Flight

Let's simulate the flight of a baseball that is batted from home plate at an angle of 45° and initial speed of 40 m/s. We'll use the center of home plate as the origin, a horizontal *x*-axis (parallel to the ground), and a vertical *y*-axis (perpendicular to the ground). The initial height is 1 m.

Here's a Params object with the parameters we'll need:

```
params = Params(
    x=0, # m
    y=1, # m
    angle=45, # degree
    speed=40, # m / s

    mass=145e-3, # kg
    diameter=73e-3, # m
    C_d=0.33, # dimensionless

    rho=1.2, # kg/m**3
    g=9.8, # m/s**2
    t_end=10, # s
)
```

I got the mass and diameter of the baseball from Wikipedia (*https://en.wikipedia.org/wiki/Baseball_(ball)*) and the coefficient of drag from *The Physics of Baseball*. The density of air, rho, is based on a temperature of 20°C at sea level (*https://en.wikipedia.org/wiki/Density_of_air#Temperature_and_pressure*). As usual, g is acceleration due to gravity. t_end is 10 seconds, which is long enough for the ball to land on the ground.

The following function uses these quantities to make a System object:

```
from numpy import pi, deg2rad

def make_system(params):

    # convert angle to radians
    theta = deg2rad(params.angle)

    # compute x and y components of velocity
    vx, vy = pol2cart(theta, params.speed)

    # make the initial state
    init = State(x=params.x, y=params.y, vx=vx, vy=vy)

    # compute the frontal area
    area = pi * (params.diameter/2)**2

    return System(params,
                  init=init,
                  area=area)
```

make_system uses deg2rad to convert angle to radians and pol2cart to compute the x and y components of the initial velocity.

init is a State object with four state variables: x and y are the components of position; vx and vy are the components of velocity.

When we call System, we pass params as the first argument, which means that the variables in params are copied to the new System object.

Here's how we make the System object:

```
system = make_system(params)
```

and here's the initial State:

```
show(system.init)
```
- -

	state
x	0.000000
y	1.000000
vx	28.284271
vy	28.284271

Now let's turn to drag.

Drag Force

We need a function to compute drag force:

```python
def drag_force(V, system):
    rho, C_d, area = system.rho, system.C_d, system.area

    mag = rho * vector_mag(V)**2 * C_d * area / 2
    direction = -vector_hat(V)
    f_drag = mag * direction
    return f_drag
```

This function takes V as a Vector and returns f_drag as a Vector.

- It uses vector_mag to compute the magnitude of V, and the drag equation to compute the magnitude of the drag force, mag.

- Then it uses vector_hat to compute direction, which is a unit vector in the opposite direction of V.

- Finally, it computes the drag force vector by multiplying mag and direction.

We can test it like this:

```python
vx, vy = system.init.vx, system.init.vy
V_test = Vector(vx, vy)
f_drag = drag_force(V_test, system)
show(f_drag)
```

	component
x	–0.937574
y	–0.937574

The result is a Vector that represents the drag force on the baseball, in newtons, under the initial conditions.

Now we can add drag to the slope function:

```python
def slope_func(t, state, system):
    x, y, vx, vy = state
    mass, g = system.mass, system.g

    V = Vector(vx, vy)
    a_drag = drag_force(V, system) / mass
    a_grav = g * Vector(0, -1)

    A = a_grav + a_drag

    return V.x, V.y, A.x, A.y
```

As usual, the parameters of the slope function are a timestamp, a State object, and a System object. We don't use t in this example, but we can't leave it out because when run_solve_ivp calls the slope function, it always provides the same arguments, whether they are needed or not.

slope_func unpacks the State object into variables x, y, vx, and vy. Then it packs vx and vy into a Vector, which it uses to compute acceleration due to drag, a_drag.

To represent acceleration due to gravity, it makes a Vector with magnitude g in the negative y direction.

The total acceleration of the baseball, A, is the sum of accelerations due to gravity and drag.

The return value is a sequence that contains the following:

- The components of velocity, V.x and V.y

- The components of acceleration, A.x and A.y

These components represent the slope of the state variables, because V is the derivative of position and A is the derivative of velocity.

As always, we can test the slope function by running it with the initial conditions:

```
slope_func(0, system.init, system)
```

```
(28.284271247461902, 28.2842712474619, -6.466030881564545, -16.266030881564546)
```

Using vectors to represent forces and accelerations makes the code concise, readable, and less error-prone. In particular, when we add a_grav and a_drag, the directions are likely to be correct, because they are encoded in the Vector objects.

Adding an Event Function

We're almost ready to run the simulation. The last thing we need is an event function that stops when the ball hits the ground:

```
def event_func(t, state, system):
    x, y, vx, vy = state
    return y
```

The event function takes the same parameters as the slope function, and it returns the y-coordinate of position. When the y-coordinate passes through 0, the simulation stops.

As we did with slope_func, we can test event_func with the initial conditions:

```
event_func(0, system.init, system)
```

```
1.0
```

Here's how we run the simulation with this event function:

```
results, details = run_solve_ivp(system, slope_func,
                                 events=event_func)
details.message
```

```
'A termination event occurred.'
```

The message indicates that a "termination event" occurred; that is, the simulated ball reached the ground.

results is a TimeFrame with one row for each time step and one column for each of the state variables. Here are the last few rows:

```
results.tail()
```
---

	x	y	vx	vy
4.804692	96.438515	4.284486	14.590855	–20.726780
4.854740	97.166460	3.238415	14.484772	–21.065476
4.904789	97.889087	2.175515	14.378566	–21.400392
4.954838	98.606374	1.095978	14.272264	–21.731499
5.004887	99.318296	0.000000	14.165894	–22.058763

We can get the flight time like this:

```
flight_time = results.index[-1]
flight_time
```

```
5.004887034868346
```

and the final state like this:

```
final_state = results.iloc[-1]
show(final_state)
```

	5.004887
x	99.318296
y	0.000000
vx	14.165894
vy	–22.058763

The final value of y is 0 or close to it, as it should be. The final value of x tells us how far the ball flew, in meters:

```
x_dist = final_state.x
x_dist
```

```
99.31829628352207
```

We can also get the final velocity, like this:

```
final_V = Vector(final_state.vx, final_state.vy)
show(final_V)
```

	component
x	14.165894
y	−22.058763

The magnitude of final velocity is the speed of the ball when it lands:

```
vector_mag(final_V)
```

```
26.215674453237572
```

The final speed is about 26 m/s, which is substantially slower than the initial speed, 40 m/s.

Visualizing Trajectories

To visualize the results, we can plot the x and y components of position like this:

```
results.x.plot(color='C4')
results.y.plot(color='C2', style='--')

decorate(xlabel='Time (s)',
         ylabel='Position (m)')
```

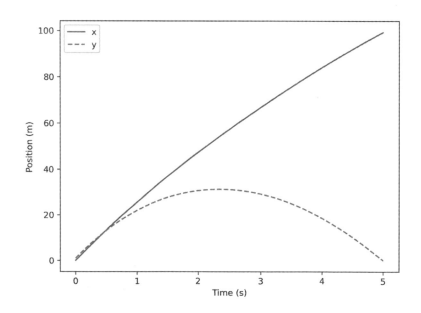

As expected, the x component increases as the ball moves away from home plate. The y position climbs initially and then descends, falling to 0 m near 5.0 s.

Another way to view the results is to plot the x component on the x-axis and the y component on the y-axis, so the plotted line follows the trajectory of the ball through the plane:

```
def plot_trajectory(results):
    x = results.x
    y = results.y
    make_series(x, y).plot(label='trajectory')

    decorate(xlabel='x position (m)',
             ylabel='y position (m)')

plot_trajectory(results)
```

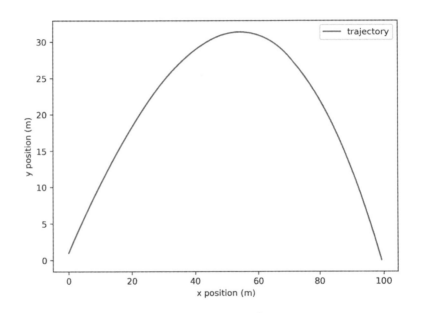

This way of visualizing the results is called a *trajectory plot*. A trajectory plot can be easier to interpret than a time series plot, because it shows what the motion of the projectile would look like (at least from one point of view). Both plots can be useful, but don't get them mixed up! If you are looking at a time series plot and interpreting it as a trajectory, you will be very confused.

Notice that the trajectory is not symmetric. With a launch angle of 45°, the landing angle is closer to vertical, about 57°.

```
rad2deg(vector_angle(final_V))
```

```
-57.29187097821225
```

Animating the Baseball

One of the best ways to visualize the results of a physical model is animation. If there are problems with the model, animation can make them apparent.

The ModSim library provides `animate`, which takes as parameters a `TimeSeries` and a draw function. The draw function should take as parameters a timestamp and a `State`. It should draw a single frame of the animation:

```
from matplotlib.pyplot import plot

xlim = results.x.min(), results.x.max()
ylim = results.y.min(), results.y.max()

def draw_func(t, state):
    plot(state.x, state.y, 'bo')
    decorate(xlabel='x position (m)',
            ylabel='y position (m)',
            xlim=xlim,
            ylim=ylim)
```

Inside the draw function, you should use `decorate` to set the limits of the x- and y-axes. Otherwise, `matplotlib` auto-scales the axes, which is usually not what you want.

Now we can run the animation like this:

```
animate(results, draw_func)
```

To run the animation, uncomment the following line of code and run the cell:

```
# animate(results, draw_func)
```

Summary

This chapter introduced `Vector` objects, which we used to represent position, velocity, and acceleration in two dimensions. We also represented forces using vectors, which make it easier to add up forces acting in different directions.

Our ODE solver doesn't work with `Vector` objects, so it takes some work to pack and unpack their components. Nevertheless, we were able to run simulations with vectors and display the results.

In the next chapter, we'll use these simulations to solve an optimization problem.

Exercises

22.1

Run the simulation with and without air resistance. How wrong would we be if we ignored drag?

22.2

The baseball stadium in Denver, Colorado, is 1,580 m above sea level, where the density of air is about 1.0 kg/m^3. Compared with the example near sea level, how much farther would a ball travel if hit with the same initial speed and launch angle?

22.3

The model so far is based on the assumption that coefficient of drag does not depend on velocity, but in reality, it does. In *The Physics of Baseball*, one of the figures shows "the drag coefficient vs. ball velocity for various balls the size of a baseball at sea level and a temperature of 68°F."

I used an online graph digitizer to extract the data from the figure and save it in a CSV file (*https://github.com/AllenDowney/ModSim/raw/main/data/baseball_drag.csv*). Figure 22-1 shows the results.

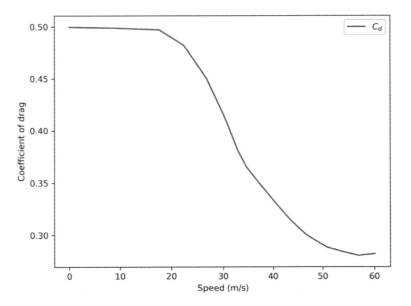

Figure 22-1: Coefficient of drag as a function of velocity

Using this data, modify the model to include the dependence of C_d on velocity, and see how much it affects the results.

23

OPTIMIZATION

In the previous chapter, we developed a model of the flight of a baseball, including gravity and a simple version of drag, but neglecting spin, Magnus force, and the dependence of the coefficient of drag on velocity.

In this chapter, we'll apply that model to an optimization problem. In general, *optimization* is a process for improving a design by searching for the parameters that maximize a benefit or minimize a cost. For example, in this chapter we'll find the angle you should hit a baseball to maximize the distance it travels. And we'll use a new function called `maximize_scalar` that searches for this angle efficiently.

This chapter is available as a Jupyter notebook where you can read the text, run the code, and work on the exercise. You can access the notebooks at *https://allendowney.github.io/ModSimPy*.

The Manny Ramirez Problem

Manny Ramirez is a former member of the Boston Red Sox (an American baseball team) who was notorious for his relaxed attitude and taste for practical jokes. Our objective in this chapter is to solve the following Manny-inspired problem:

What is the minimum effort required to hit a home run in Fenway Park?

Fenway Park is a baseball stadium in Boston, Massachusetts. One of its most famous features is the "Green Monster," which is a wall in left field that is unusually close to home plate, only 310 feet away. To compensate for the short distance, the wall is unusually high, at 37 feet (*https://en.wikipedia.org/wiki/Green_Monster*).

Starting with params from the previous chapter, we'll make a new Params object with two additional parameters, wall_distance and wall_height, in meters:

```
feet_to_meter = (1 * units.feet).to(units.meter).magnitude

params = params.set(
    wall_distance=310 * feet_to_meter,
    wall_height=37 * feet_to_meter
)

show(params)
```

---

	value
x	0.0000
y	1.0000
angle	45.0000
speed	40.0000
mass	0.1450
diameter	0.0730
C_d	0.3300
rho	1.2000
g	9.8000
t_end	10.0000
wall_distance	94.4880
wall_height	11.2776

The answer we want is the minimum speed at which a ball can leave home plate and still go over the Green Monster. We'll proceed in the following steps:

1. For a given speed, we'll find the optimal *launch angle*, that is, the angle the ball should leave home plate to maximize its height when it reaches the wall.

2. Then we'll find the minimum speed that clears the wall, given that it has the optimal launch angle.

Finding the Range

Suppose we want to find the launch angle that maximizes *range*, that is, the distance the ball travels in the air before landing. We'll use a function in the ModSim library, maximize_scalar, which takes a function and finds its maximum.

The function we pass to maximize_scalar should take launch angle in degrees, simulate the flight of a ball launched at that angle, and return the distance the ball travels along the x-axis:

```
def range_func(angle, params):
    params = params.set(angle=angle)
    system = make_system(params)
    results, details = run_solve_ivp(system, slope_func,
                                     events=event_func)
    x_dist = results.iloc[-1].x
    print(angle, x_dist)
    return x_dist
```

range_func makes a new System object with the given value of angle. Then it calls run_solve_ivp and returns the final value of x from the results.

We can call range_func directly like this:

```
range_func(45, params)
```

```
45 99.31829628352207
99.31829628352207
```

With launch angle 45°, the ball lands about 99 m from home plate.

Now we can sweep a sequence of angles like this:

```
angles = linspace(20, 80, 21)
sweep = SweepSeries()

for angle in angles:
    x_dist = range_func(angle, params)
    sweep[angle] = x_dist
```

```
20.0 78.09741067882733
23.0 84.11542610650983
26.0 89.13192412363966
29.0 93.17466724082834
--snip--
74.0 51.402871099404315
77.0 42.72047925533483
80.0 33.48437980813934
```

Here's what the results look like:

```
sweep.plot()

decorate(xlabel='Launch angle (degrees)',
         ylabel='Range (m)')
```

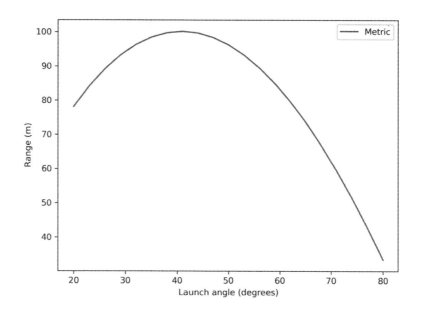

It looks like the range is maximized when the initial angle is near $40°$.

We can find the optimal angle more precisely and more efficiently using maximize_scalar, like this:

```
res = maximize_scalar(range_func, params, bounds=[0, 90])
```

```
0 17.468795355645696
34.37694101250946 98.06996498016366
55.62305898749054 90.03182421721928
21.246117974981075 80.72039493627986
41.173855871044005 100.1200188931698
40.980120907838035 100.12368377099199
```

```
40.882137319070246 100.1241700443184
40.87925420124324 100.12417043309694
40.87928713865314 100.12417043314977
40.879291078324286 100.12417043314917
40.879283198981994 100.12417043314895
```

The first parameter is the function we want to maximize. The second is the range of values we want to search; in this case, it's the range of angles from 0° to 90°.

The return value from `maximize_scalar` is an object that contains the results:

```
res
```

```
     fun: 100.12417043314977
 message: 'Solution found.'
    nfev: 10
  status: 0
 success: True
       x: 40.87928713865314
```

It includes `x`, which is the angle that yielded the maximum range, and `fun`, which is the range when the ball is launched at the optimal angle:

```
res.x, res.fun
```
- -
```
(40.87928713865314, 100.12417043314977)
```

For these parameters, the optimal angle is about 41°, which yields a range of 100 m. Now we have what we need to finish the problem; the last step is to find the minimum velocity needed to get the ball over the wall. In the exercise at the end of the chapter, I provide some suggestions. Then it's up to you!

Summary

This chapter introduced a new tool, `maximize_scalar`, that provides an efficient way to search for the maximum of a function. We used it to find the launch angle that maximizes the distance a baseball flies through the air, given its initial velocity.

If you enjoyed this example, you might be interested in this paper by Sawicki, Hubbard, and Stronge: "How to Hit Home Runs: Optimum Baseball Bat Swing Parameters for Maximum Range Trajectories" (see *https:// aapt.scitation.org/doi/abs/10.1119/1.1604384*).

In the next chapter, we start a new topic: rotation!

Exercise

23.1

Let's finish off the Manny Ramirez problem:

> What is the minimum effort required to hit a home run in Fenway Park?

Although the problem asks for a minimum, it is not an optimization problem. Rather, we want to solve for the initial speed that just barely gets the ball to the top of the wall, given that it is launched at the optimal angle. And we have to be careful about what we mean by "optimal." For this problem, we don't want the longest range; we want the maximum height at the point where it reaches the wall.

If you are ready to solve the problem on your own, go ahead. Otherwise, I will walk you through the process with an outline and some starter code.

As a first step, write an event_func that stops the simulation when the ball reaches the wall at wall_distance, which is a parameter in params. Test your function with the initial conditions.

Next, write a function called height_func that takes a launch angle, simulates the flight of a baseball, and returns the height of the baseball when it reaches the wall. Test your function with the initial conditions.

Now use maximize_scalar to find the optimal angle. Is it higher or lower than the angle that maximizes range?

The angle that maximizes the height at the wall is a little higher than the angle that maximizes range.

Now, let's find the initial speed that makes the height at the wall exactly 37 feet, given that the ball is launched at the optimal angle. This is a root-finding problem, so we'll use root_scalar.

Write an error function that takes a speed and a System object as parameters. It should use maximize_scalar to find the highest possible height of the ball at the wall, for the given speed. Then it should return the difference between that optimal height and wall_height, which is a parameter in params.

Test your error function before you call root_scalar. Then use root_scalar to find the answer to the problem: the minimum speed that gets the ball out of the park. And just to check, run error_func with the value you found.

Under the Hood

maximize_scalar uses a SciPy function called minimize_scalar, which provides several optimization methods. By default, it uses bounded, a version of Brent's algorithm that is safe in the sense that it always uses values within the bounds you provide (including both ends). You can read more about it at *https://en.wikipedia.org/wiki/Golden-section_search*.

24

ROTATION

In this chapter and the next, we'll model systems that involve rotating objects. In general, rotation is complicated. In three dimensions, objects can rotate around three axes, and many objects are easier to spin around some axes than others. If the configuration of an object changes over time, it might become easier or harder to spin, which explains the surprising dynamics of gymnasts, divers, ice skaters, and so on. When you apply a twisting force to a rotating object, the effect is often contrary to intuition. For an example, see this video on gyroscopic precession: *https://www.youtube.com/watch?v=ty9QSiVC2g0*.

We will not take on the physics of rotation in all its glory; rather, we will focus on simple scenarios where all rotation and all twisting forces are around a single axis. In such cases, we can treat some vector quantities as if they were scalars—that is, simple numbers.

The fundamental ideas in these examples are angular velocity, angular acceleration, torque, and moment of inertia. If you are not already familiar with these concepts, don't worry; I will define them as we go along, and I will point to additional reading.

This chapter is available as a Jupyter notebook where you can read the text, run the code, and work on the exercise. You can access the notebooks at *https://allendowney.github.io/ModSimPy*.

The Physics of Toilet Paper

As an example of a system with rotation, we'll simulate the manufacture of a roll of toilet paper, as shown in this video: *https://youtu.be/Z74OfpUbeac? t=231*. Starting with a cardboard tube at the center, we will roll up 47 m of paper, a typical length for a roll of toilet paper in the United States (*https://en.wikipedia.org/wiki/Toilet_paper*).

Figure 24-1 shows a diagram of the system: r represents the radius of the roll at a point in time. Initially, r is the radius of the cardboard core, R_{min}. When the roll is complete, r is R_{max}.

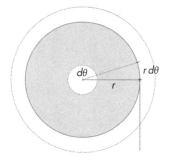

Figure 24-1: A diagram of a roll of toilet paper, showing change in paper length as a result of a small rotation, $d\theta$

I'll use θ to represent the total rotation of the roll in radians. In the diagram, $d\theta$ represents a small increase in θ, which corresponds to a distance along the circumference of $r\,d\theta$.

I'll use y to represent the total length of paper that's been rolled. Initially, $\theta = 0$ and $y = 0$. For each small increase in θ, there is a corresponding increase in y:

$$dy = r\,d\theta$$

If we divide both sides by a small increase in time, dt, we get a differential equation for y as a function of time:

$$\frac{dy}{dt} = r\frac{d\theta}{dt}$$

As we roll up the paper, r increases. Assuming it increases by a fixed amount per revolution, we can write:

$$dr = k \, d\theta$$

where k is an unknown constant we'll have to figure out. Again, we can divide both sides by dt to get a differential equation in time:

$$\frac{dr}{dt} = k\frac{d\theta}{dt}$$

Finally, let's assume that θ increases at a constant rate of $\omega = 300$ rad/s (about 2,900 revolutions per minute):

$$\frac{d\theta}{dt} = \omega$$

This rate of change is called an *angular velocity*. Now we have a system of differential equations we can use to simulate the system.

Setting Parameters

Here are the parameters of the system:

```
Rmin = 0.02 # m
Rmax = 0.055 # m
L = 47 # m
omega = 300 # rad/s
```

Rmin and Rmax are the initial and final values for the radius, r. L is the total length of the paper. omega is the angular velocity in radians per second.

Figuring out k is not easy, but we can estimate it by pretending that r is constant and equal to the average of Rmin and Rmax:

```
Ravg = (Rmax + Rmin) / 2
```

In that case, the circumference of the roll is also constant:

```
Cavg = 2 * np.pi * Ravg
```

We can compute the number of revolutions to roll up length L, like this:

```
revs = L / Cavg
```

Converting rotations to radians, we can estimate the final value of theta:

```
theta = 2 * np.pi * revs
theta
```

```
1253.3333333333335
```

Finally, k is the total change in r divided by the total change in theta:

```
k_est = (Rmax - Rmin) / theta
k_est
```

```
2.7925531914893616e-05
```

At the end of the chapter, we'll derive k analytically, but this estimate is enough to get started.

Simulating the System

The state variables we'll use are theta, y, and r. The initial conditions are:

```
init = State(theta=0, y=0, r=Rmin)
```

and here's a System object with init and t_end:

```
system = System(init=init, t_end=10)
```

Now we can use the differential equations from "The Physics of Toilet Paper" section to write a slope function:

```
def slope_func(t, state, system):
    theta, y, r = state

    dydt = r * omega
    drdt = k_est * omega

    return omega, dydt, drdt
```

As usual, the slope function takes a timestamp, a State object, and a System object.

The job of the slope function is to compute the time derivatives of the state variables. The derivative of theta is angular velocity, omega. The derivatives of y and r are given by the differential equations we derived.

And as usual, we'll test the slope function with the initial conditions:

```
slope_func(0, system.init, system)
```

```
(300, 6.0, 0.008377659574468085)
```

We'd like to stop the simulation when the length of paper on the roll is L. We can do that with an event function that passes through 0 when y equals L:

```
def event_func(t, state, system):
    theta, y, r = state
    return L - y
```

We can test it with the initial conditions:

```
event_func(0, system.init, system)
```

```
47.0
```

Now let's run the simulation:

```
results, details = run_solve_ivp(system, slope_func,
                                 events=event_func)
details.message
```

```
'A termination event occurred.'
```

Here are the last few time steps:

```
results.tail()
```

	theta	y	r
4.010667	1203.200000	44.277760	0.05360
4.052444	1215.733333	44.951740	0.05395
4.094222	1228.266667	45.630107	0.05430
4.136000	1240.800000	46.312860	0.05465
4.177778	1253.333333	47.000000	0.05500

The time it takes to complete one roll is about 4.2 seconds, which is consistent with what we see in the video:

```
results.index[-1]
```

```
4.177777777777779
```

The final value of y is 47 m, as expected:

```
final_state = results.iloc[-1]
final_state.y
```

```
47.00000000000001
```

The final value of r is 0.55 m, which is Rmax:

```
final_state.r
```

```
0.05500000000000001
```

The total number of rotations is close to 200, which seems plausible:

```
radians = final_state.theta
rotations = radians / 2 / np.pi
rotations
```

199.47419534184218

As an exercise, we'll see how fast the paper is moving. But first, let's take a closer look at the results.

Plotting the Results

Here's what theta looks like over time:

```
def plot_theta(results):
    results.theta.plot(color='C0', label='theta')
    decorate(xlabel='Time (s)',
             ylabel='Angle (rad)')


plot_theta(results)
```

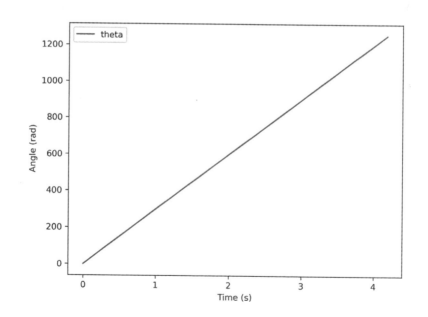

theta grows linearly, as we should expect with constant angular velocity.

Here's what r looks like over time:

```
def plot_r(results):
    results.r.plot(color='C2', label='r')

    decorate(xlabel='Time (s)',
             ylabel='Radius (m)')

plot_r(results)
```

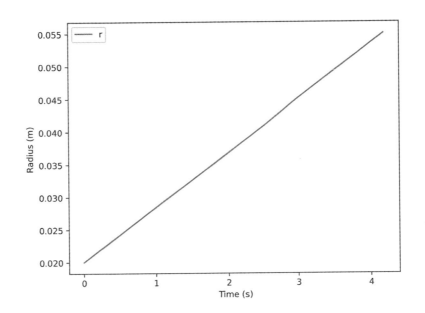

r also increases linearly.

Here's what y looks like over time:

```
def plot_y(results):
    results.y.plot(color='C1', label='y')

    decorate(xlabel='Time (s)',
             ylabel='Length (m)')

plot_y(results)
```

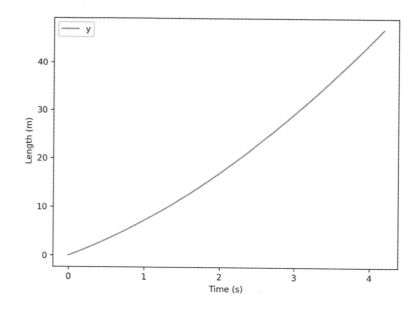

Since the derivative of y depends on r, and r is increasing, y grows with increasing slope.

In the next section, we'll see that we could have solved these differential equations analytically. However, it is often useful to start with simulation as a way of exploring and checking assumptions.

The Analytic Solution

Since angular velocity is constant:

$$\frac{d\theta}{dt} = \omega \quad (1)$$

we can find θ as a function of time by integrating both sides:

$$\theta(t) = \omega t$$

Similarly, we can solve

$$\frac{dr}{dt} = k\omega$$

to find

$$r(t) = k\omega t + R_{min}$$

and then we can plug the solution for r into the equation for y:

$$\frac{dy}{dt} = r\omega \quad (2)$$

$$= \left[k\omega t + R_{min}\right]\omega$$

Integrating both sides yields:

$$y(t) = \left[k\omega t^2/2 + R_{min}t\right]\omega$$

So y is a parabola, as you might have guessed.

We can also use these equations to find the relationship between y and r, independent of time, which we can use to compute k. Dividing Equations 1 and 2 yields:

$$\frac{dr}{dy} = \frac{k}{r}$$

Separating variables yields:

$$r \, dr = k \, dy$$

Integrating both sides yields:

$$r^2/2 = ky + C$$

Solving for y, we have:

$$y = \frac{1}{2k}(r^2 - C)$$

When $y = 0$, $r = R_{min}$, so:

$$R_{min}^2/2 = C$$

When $y = L$, $r = R_{max}$, so:

$$L = \frac{1}{2k}(R_{max}^2 - R_{min}^2)$$

Solving for k yields:

$$k = \frac{1}{2L}(R_{max}^2 - R_{min}^2)$$

Plugging in the values of the parameters yields 2.8e-5 m/rad, the same as the "estimate" we computed in "The Physics of Toilet Paper":

```
k = (Rmax**2 - Rmin**2) / (2 * L)
k
```

```
2.7925531914893616e-05
```

In this case the estimate turns out to be exact.

Summary

This chapter introduced rotation, starting with an example where angular velocity is constant. We simulated the manufacture of a roll of toilet paper, then we solved the same problem analytically.

In the next chapter, we'll see a more interesting example where angular velocity is not constant. And we'll introduce three new concepts: torque, angular acceleration, and moment of inertia.

Exercise

24.1

Since we keep `omega` constant, the linear velocity of the paper increases with radius. We can use `gradient` to estimate the derivative of `results.y`:

```
dydt = gradient(results.y)
```

Here's what the result looks like:

```
dydt.plot(label='dydt')
decorate(xlabel='Time (s)',
        ylabel='Linear velocity (m/s)')
```

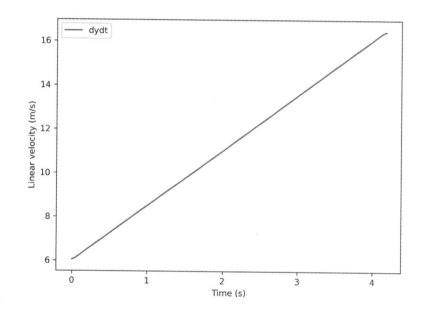

With constant angular velocity, linear velocity is increasing, reaching its maximum at the end:

```
max_linear_velocity = dydt.iloc[-1]
max_linear_velocity
```
- -
```
16.447499999999934
```

Now suppose this peak velocity is the limiting factor; that is, we can't move the paper any faster than that. In that case, we might be able to speed up the process by keeping the linear velocity at the maximum all the time.

Write a slope function that keeps the linear velocity, `dydt`, constant and computes the angular velocity, `omega`, accordingly. Then, run the simulation and see how much faster we could finish rolling the paper.

25

TORQUE

In the previous chapter, we modeled a system with constant angular velocity. In this chapter, we'll take the next step, modeling a system with angular acceleration and deceleration.

This chapter is available as a Jupyter notebook where you can read the text, run the code, and work on the exercise. You can access the notebooks at *https://allendowney.github.io/ModSimPy*.

Angular Acceleration

Just as linear acceleration is the derivative of velocity, *angular acceleration* is the derivative of angular velocity. And just as linear acceleration is caused by force, angular acceleration is caused by the rotational version of force, *torque*. In general, torque is a vector quantity, defined as the *cross product* of $\vec{r}$ and $\vec{F}$, where $\vec{r}$ is the *lever arm*, a vector from the center of rotation to the point where the force is applied, and $\vec{F}$ is the vector that represents the magnitude and direction of the force.

For the problems in this chapter, however, we only need the *magnitude* of torque; we don't care about the direction. In that case, we can compute this product of scalar quantities:

$$\tau = rF\sin\theta$$

where τ is torque, r is the length of the lever arm, F is the magnitude of force, and θ is the angle between $\vec{r}$ and $\vec{F}$.

Since torque is the product of a length and a force, it is expressed in newton meters (N m).

Moment of Inertia

In the same way that linear acceleration is related to force by Newton's second law of motion, $F = ma$, angular acceleration is related to torque by another form of Newton's law:

$$\tau = I\alpha$$

where α is angular acceleration and I is *moment of inertia*. Just as mass is what makes it hard to accelerate an object, moment of inertia is what makes it hard to spin an object.

In the most general case—a three-dimensional object rotating around an arbitrary axis—moment of inertia is a *tensor*, which is a function that takes a vector as a parameter and returns a vector as a result.

Fortunately, in a system where all rotation and torque happens around a single axis, we don't have to deal with the most general case. We can treat moment of inertia as a scalar quantity.

For a small object with mass m, rotating around a point at distance r, the moment of inertia is $I = mr^2$. For more complex objects, we can compute I by dividing the object into small masses, computing moments of inertia for each mass, and adding them up. For most simple shapes, people have already done the calculations; you can just look up the answers. For example, see *https://en.wikipedia.org/wiki/List_of_moments_of_inertia*.

Teapots and Turntables

Tables in Chinese restaurants often have a rotating tray or turntable that makes it easy for customers to share dishes. These turntables are supported by low-friction bearings that allow them to turn easily and glide. However, they can be heavy, especially when they are loaded with food, so they have a high moment of inertia.

Suppose I am sitting at a table with a pot of tea on the turntable directly in front of me, and the person sitting directly opposite asks me to pass the tea. I push on the edge of the turntable with 2 N of force until it has turned 0.5 rad, then let go. The turntable glides until it comes to a stop 1.5 rad from the starting position. How much force should I apply for a second push so the teapot glides to a stop directly opposite me?

We'll answer this question in these steps:

1. We'll use the results from the first push to estimate the coefficient of friction for the turntable.

2. As an exercise, you'll use that coefficient of friction to estimate the force needed to rotate the turntable through the remaining angle.

Our simulation will use the following parameters:

1. The radius of the turntable is 0.5 m, and its weight is 7 kg.

2. The teapot weights 0.3 kg, and it sits 0.4 m from the center of the turntable.

Figure 25-1 shows the scenario, where F is the force I apply to the turntable at the perimeter, perpendicular to the lever arm, r, and τ is the resulting torque. The circle near the bottom is the teapot.

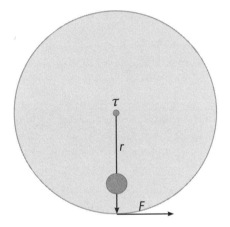

Figure 25-1: A diagram of a teapot on a turntable showing the force, the lever arm, and the resulting torque

Here are the parameters from the statement of the problem:

```
from numpy import pi

radius_disk = 0.5 # m
mass_disk = 7 # kg
radius_pot = 0.4 # m
mass_pot = 0.3 # kg
force = 2 # N

theta_push = 0.5 # radian
theta_test = 1.5 # radian
theta_target = pi # radian
```

theta_push is the angle where I stop pushing on the turntable. theta_test is how far the table turns during my test push. theta_target is where we want the table to be after the second push.

We can use these parameters to compute the moment of inertia of the turntable, using the formula for a horizontal disk revolving around a vertical axis through its center:

```
I_disk = mass_disk * radius_disk**2 / 2
```

We can also compute the moment of inertia of the teapot, treating it as a point mass:

```
I_pot = mass_pot * radius_pot**2
```

The total moment of inertia is the sum of these parts:

```
I_total = I_disk + I_pot
```

Friction in the bearings probably depends on the weight of the turntable and its contents, but it probably does not depend on angular velocity. So we'll assume that it is a constant. We don't know what it is, so we will start with a guess, and we will use root_scalar later to improve it:

```
torque_friction = 0.3 # N*m
```

For this problem we'll treat friction as a torque.

The state variables we'll use are theta, which is the angle of the table in radians, and omega, which is angular velocity in radians per second:

```
init = State(theta=0, omega=0)
```

Now we can make a System with the initial state, init, the maximum duration of the simulation, t_end, and the parameters we are going to vary, force and torque_friction:

```
system = System(init=init,
                force=force,
                torque_friction=torque_friction,
                t_end=20)
```

Here's a slope function that takes the current state, which contains angle and angular velocity, and returns the derivatives, angular velocity and angular acceleration:

```
def slope_func(t, state, system):
    theta, omega = state
    force = system.force
    torque_friction = system.torque_friction

    torque = radius_disk * force - torque_friction
    alpha = torque / I_total

    return omega, alpha
```

In this scenario, the force I apply to the turntable is always perpendicular to the lever arm, so $\sin\theta = 1$ and the torque due to force is $\tau = rF$.

torque_friction represents the torque due to friction. Because the turntable is rotating in the direction of positive theta, friction acts in the direction of negative theta.

We can test the slope function with the initial conditions:

```
slope_func(0, system.init, system)
```
```
(0, 0.7583965330444203)
```

We are almost ready to run the simulation, but first there's a problem we have to address.

Two-Phase Simulation

When I stop pushing on the turntable, the angular acceleration changes abruptly. We could implement the slope function with an if statement that checks the value of theta and sets force accordingly. And for a coarse model like this one, that might be fine. But a more robust approach is to simulate the system in two phases:

1. During the first phase, force is constant, and we run until theta is 0.5 rad.

2. During the second phase, force is 0, and we run until omega is 0.

Then we can combine the results of the two phases into a single TimeFrame.

Phase 1

Here's the event function we'll use for Phase 1; it stops the simulation when theta reaches theta_push, which is when I stop pushing:

```
def event_func1(t, state, system):
    theta, omega = state
    return theta - theta_push
```

We can test it with the initial conditions:

```
event_func1(0, system.init, system)
```

```
-0.5
```

and run the first phase of the simulation:

```
results1, details1 = run_solve_ivp(system, slope_func,
                                    events=event_func1)
details1.message
```

```
'A termination event occurred.'
```

Here are the last few time steps:

```
results1.tail()
```

	theta	omega
1.102359	0.46080	0.836025
1.113842	0.47045	0.844734
1.125325	0.48020	0.853442
1.136808	0.49005	0.862151
1.148291	0.50000	0.870860

It takes a little more than a second for me to rotate the table 0.5 rad. When I release the table, the angular velocity is about 0.87 rad/s.

Before we run the second phase, we have to extract the final time and state of the first phase:

```
t_2 = results1.index[-1]
init2 = results1.iloc[-1]
```

Phase 2

Now we can make a System object for Phase 2 with the initial state from Phase 1 and with force=0:

```
system2 = system.set(t_0=t_2, init=init2, force=0)
```

For the second phase, we need an event function that stops when the turntable stops—that is, when angular velocity is 0:

```
def event_func2(t, state, system):
    theta, omega = state
    return omega
```

We'll test it with the initial conditions for Phase 2:

```
event_func2(system2.t_0, system2.init, system2)
```

```
0.8708596517490182
```

The result is the angular velocity at the beginning of Phase 2, in radians per second.

Now we can run the second phase:

```
results2, details2 = run_solve_ivp(system2, slope_func,
                                   events=event_func2)

details2.message
```

```
'A termination event occurred.'
```

Let's put it all together.

Combining the Results

DataFrame provides append, which appends results2 to the end of results1:

```
results = results1.append(results2)
```

Here are the last few time steps:

```
results.tail()
```

	theta	omega
3.720462	1.664800	3.483439e–02
3.747255	1.665617	2.612579e–02
3.774049	1.666200	1.741719e–02
3.800842	1.666550	8.708597e–03
3.827636	1.666667	–2.220446e–16

At the end, angular velocity is close to 0, and the total rotation is about 1.7 rad, a little farther than we were aiming for.

We can plot theta for both phases:

```
results.theta.plot(label='theta')
decorate(xlabel='Time (s)',
         ylabel='Angle (rad)')
```

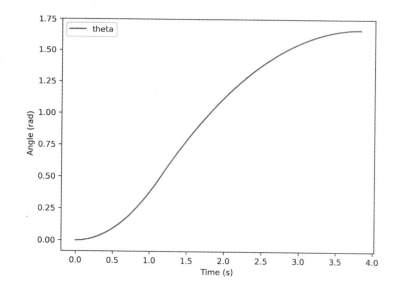

and omega:

```
results.omega.plot(label='omega', color='C1')
decorate(xlabel='Time (s)',
         ylabel='Angular velocity (rad/s)')
```

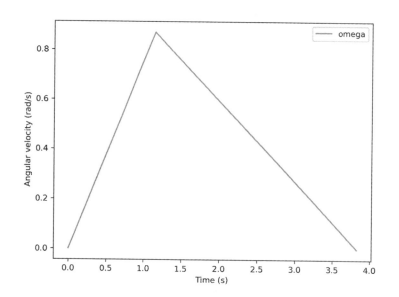

Angular velocity, omega, increases linearly while I am pushing, and decreases linearly after I let go. The angle, theta, is the integral of angular velocity, so it forms a parabola during each phase.

In the next section, we'll use this simulation to estimate the torque due to friction.

Estimating Friction

Let's take the code from the previous section and wrap it in a function:

```
def run_two_phases(force, torque_friction, system):

    # put the specified parameters into the System object
    system1 = system.set(force=force,
                          torque_friction=torque_friction)

    # run phase 1
    results1, details1 = run_solve_ivp(system1, slope_func,
                                        events=event_func1)

    # get the final state from phase 1
    t_2 = results1.index[-1]
    init2 = results1.iloc[-1]

    # run phase 2
    system2 = system1.set(t_0=t_2, init=init2, force=0)
    results2, details2 = run_solve_ivp(system2, slope_func,
                                        events=event_func2)

    # combine and return the results
    results = results1.append(results2)
    return results
```

We'll test it with the same parameters:

```
force = 2
torque_friction = 0.3
results = run_two_phases(force, torque_friction, system)
results.tail()
```

	theta	omega
3.720462	1.664800	3.483439e-02
3.747255	1.665617	2.612579e-02
3.774049	1.666200	1.741719e-02
3.800842	1.666550	8.708597e-03
3.827636	1.666667	-2.220446e-16

These results are the same as in the previous section.

We can use run_two_phases to write an error function we can use, with root_scalar, to find the torque due to friction that yields the observed results from the first push, a total rotation of 1.5 rad.

```
def error_func1(torque_friction, system):
    force = system.force
```

```
results = run_two_phases(force, torque_friction, system)
theta_final = results.iloc[-1].theta
print(torque_friction, theta_final)
return theta_final - theta_test
```

This error function takes torque due to friction as an input. It extracts force from the System object and runs the simulation. From the results, it extracts the last value of theta and returns the difference between the result of the simulation and the result of the experiment. When this difference is 0, the value of torque_friction is an estimate for the friction in the experiment.

To bracket the root, we need one value that's too low and one that's too high. With torque_friction=0.3, the table rotates a bit too far:

```
guess1 = 0.3
error_func1(guess1, system)
```

```
0.3 1.666666666666669
0.16666666666666896
```

With torque_friction=0.4, it doesn't go far enough:

```
guess2 = 0.4
error_func1(guess2, system)
```

```
0.4 1.2499999999999996
-0.25000000000000044
```

So we can use those two values as a bracket for root_scalar:

```
res = root_scalar(error_func1, system, bracket=[guess1, guess2])
```

```
0.3 1.666666666666669
0.3 1.666666666666669
0.4 1.2499999999999996
0.3400000000000003 1.4705882352941169
0.3340000000000002 1.4970059880239517
0.3333320000000001 1.5000060000239976
0.3333486666010001 1.4999310034693254
```

The result is 0.333 N m, a little less than the initial guess:

```
actual_friction = res.root
actual_friction
```

```
0.3333320000000001
```

Now that we know the torque due to friction, we can compute the force needed to rotate the turntable through the remaining angle, that is, from 1.5 rad to 3.14 rad. You'll have a chance to do that as an exercise, but first, let's animate the results.

Animating the Turntable

We can use animation to visualize the results of the simulation. Here's a function that takes the state of the system and draws it:

```python
from matplotlib.patches import Circle
from matplotlib.pyplot import gca, axis

def draw_func(t, state):
    theta, omega = state

    # draw a circle for the table
    circle1 = Circle([0, 0], radius_disk)
    gca().add_patch(circle1)

    # draw a circle for the teapot
    center = pol2cart(theta, radius_pot)
    circle2 = Circle(center, 0.05, color='C1')
    gca().add_patch(circle2)

    axis('equal')
```

This function uses a few features we have not seen before, but you can read about them in the Matplotlib documentation.

We can use it to show what the initial condition looks like:

```python
state = results.iloc[0]
draw_func(0, state)
```

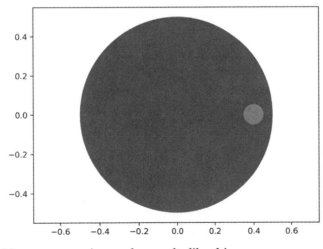

Now we can animate the results like this:

```python
animate(results, draw_func)
```

When you run this code in the Jupyter notebook, you'll be able to see the animation.

Summary

The example in this chapter demonstrated the concepts of torque, angular acceleration, and moment of inertia. We used these concepts to simulate a turntable, using a hypothetical observation to estimate torque due to friction. As an exercise, you can finish off the example, estimating the force needed to rotate the table to a given target angle.

The next chapter describes several case studies you can work on to practice the tools from the last few chapters, including projectiles, rotating objects, root_scalar, and maximize_scalar.

Exercise

25.1

Continuing the example from this chapter, estimate the force that delivers the teapot to the desired position. Use this System object, with the friction we computed in the "Estimating Friction" section:

```
system3 = system.set(torque_friction=actual_friction)
```

Write an error function that takes force and system, simulates the system, and returns the difference between theta_final and the remaining angle after the first push:

```
remaining_angle = theta_target - theta_test
remaining_angle
```

```
1.6415926535897931
```

Use your error function and root_scalar to find the force needed for the second push. Run the simulation with the force you computed and confirm that the table stops at the target angle after both pushes.

26

CASE STUDIES PART III

This chapter is a collection of case studies you might want to read and work on. They are based on the methods in the last few chapters, including Newtonian mechanics in one and two dimensions, and rotation around a single axis.

This chapter is available as a Jupyter notebook where you can read the text, run the code, and work on the case studies. You can access the notebooks at *https://allendowney.github.io/ModSimPy*.

Bungee Jumping

Suppose you want to set the world record for the highest "bungee dunk," which is a stunt in which a bungee jumper dunks a cookie in a cup of tea at the lowest point of a jump. An example is shown in this video: *https://www .youtube.com/watch?v=UBf7WC19lpw&ab_channel=OnDemandNews*.

Since the record is 70 m, let's design a jump for 80 m. We'll start with the following modeling assumptions:

- Initially the bungee cord hangs from a crane with the attachment point 80 m above a cup of tea.

- Until the cord is fully extended, it applies no force to the jumper. It turns out this might not be a good assumption; we'll revisit it in the next case study.

- After the cord is fully extended, it obeys Hooke's law; that is, it applies a force to the jumper proportional to the extension of the cord beyond its resting length.

- The mass of the jumper is 75 kg.

- The jumper is subject to drag force so that their terminal velocity is 60 m/s.

Our objective is to choose the length of the cord, L, and its spring constant, k, so that the jumper falls all the way to the tea cup, but no farther!

In the repository for this book, you will find a notebook, *bungee1.ipynb*, which contains starter code and exercises for this case study. You can download it from *https://github.com/AllenDowney/ModSimPy/raw/master/examples/bungee1.ipynb* or run it on Colab at*https://colab.research.google.com/github/AllenDowney/ModSimPy/blob/master/examples/bungee1.ipynb*.

Bungee Dunk Revisited

In the previous case study, we assumed that the cord applies no force to the jumper until it is stretched. It is tempting to say that the cord has no effect because it falls along with the jumper, but that intuition is incorrect. As the cord falls, it transfers energy to the jumper.

At *https://iopscience.iop.org/article/10.1088/0031-9120/45/1/007* you'll find a paper by Heck, Uylings, and Kedzierska, "Understanding the Physics of Bungee Jumping," that explains this phenomenon and derives the acceleration of the jumper, a, as a function of position, y, and velocity, v:

$$a = g + \frac{\mu v^2 / 2}{\mu(L + y) + 2L}$$

where g is acceleration due to gravity, L is the length of the cord, and μ is the ratio of the mass of the cord, m, and the mass of the jumper, M.

If you don't believe that their model is correct, this video might convince you: *https://www.youtube.com/watch?v=X-QFAB0gEtE*.

In the repository for this book, you will find a notebook, *bungee2.ipynb*, which contains starter code and exercises for this case study. You can download it from *https://github.com/AllenDowney/ModSimPy/raw/master/examples/bungee2.ipynb* or run it on Colab at *https://colab.research.google.com/github/AllenDowney/ModSimPy/blob/master/examples/bungee2.ipynb*.

How does the behavior of the system change as we vary the mass of the cord? When the mass of the cord equals the mass of the jumper, what is the net effect on the lowest point in the jump?

Orbiting the Sun

In the exercise at the end of Chapter 20, we modeled the interaction between the Earth and the Sun, simulating what would happen if the Earth stopped in its orbit and fell straight into the Sun. Now let's extend the model to two dimensions and simulate one revolution of the Earth around the Sun (that is, one year).

In the repository for this book, you will find a notebook, *orbit.ipynb*, which contains starter code and exercises for this case study. You can download it from *https://github.com/AllenDowney/ModSimPy/raw/master/examples/ orbit.ipynb* or run it on Colab at*https://colab.research.google.com/github/ AllenDowney/ModSimPy/blob/master/examples/orbit.ipynb*.

Among other things, you will have a chance to experiment with different algorithms and see what effect they have on the accuracy of the results.

Spider-Man

In this case study we'll develop a model of Spider-Man swinging from a springy cable of webbing attached to the top of the Empire State Building. Initially, Spider-Man is at the top of a nearby building, as shown in Figure 26-1.

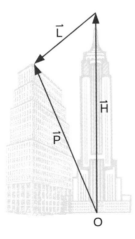

Figure 26-1: A diagram of the Spider-Man scenario with vectors representing the relative positions of the origin, Spider-Man, and the attachment point of the webbing

The origin, 0, is at the base of the Empire State Building. The vector H represents the position where the webbing is attached to the building, relative to O. The vector P is the position of Spider-Man relative to O. And L is the vector from the attachment point to Spider-Man.

By following the arrows from O, along H, and along L, we can see that:

```
H + L = P
```

So we can compute L like this:

```
L = P - H
```

The goals of this case study are as follows:

1. Implement a model of this scenario to predict Spider-Man's trajectory.

2. Choose the right time for Spider-Man to let go of the webbing in order to maximize the distance he travels before landing.

3. Choose the best angle for Spider-Man to jump off the building, and let go of the webbing, to maximize range.

We'll use the following parameters:

1. According to the Spider-Man Wiki (*https://spiderman.fandom.com/ wiki/Peter_Parker_(Earth-616)*), Spider-Man weighs 76 kg.

2. Let's assume his terminal velocity is 60 m/s.

3. The length of the web is 100 m.

4. The initial angle of the web is 45° to the left of straight down.

5. The spring constant of the web is 40 N/m when the cord is stretched, and 0 when it's compressed.

In the repository for this book, you will find a notebook, *spiderman.ipynb*, which contains starter code. You can download it from *https://github.com/ AllenDowney/ModSimPy/raw/master/examples/spiderman.ipynb* or run it on Colab at *https://colab.research.google.com/github/AllenDowney/ModSimPy/blob/ master/examples/spiderman.ipynb*.

Read through the notebook and run the code. It uses `minimize`, which is a SciPy function that can search for an optimal set of parameters (as contrasted with `minimize_scalar`, which can only search along a single axis).

Kittens

If you have used the internet, you have probably seen videos of kittens unrolling toilet paper. And you might have wondered how long it would take a standard kitten to unroll 47 m of paper, the length of a standard roll.

The interactions of the kitten and the paper roll are complex. To keep things simple, let's assume that the kitten pulls down on the free end of the roll with constant force. And let's neglect the friction between the roll and the axle.

Figure 26-2 shows the paper roll with the force applied by the kitten, F, the lever arm of the force around the axis of rotation, r, and the resulting torque, τ.

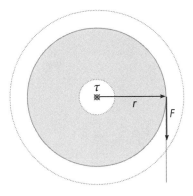

Figure 26-2: A diagram of a roll of toilet paper, showing the force, the lever arm, and the resulting torque

Assuming that the force applied by the kitten is 0.002 N, how long would it take to unroll a standard roll of toilet paper?

In the repository for this book, you will find a notebook, *kitten.ipynb*, which contains starter code for this case study. Use it to implement this model and check whether the results seem plausible. You can download it from *https://github.com/AllenDowney/ModSimPy/raw/master/examples/kitten .ipynb* or run it on Colab at *https://colab.research.google.com/github/AllenDowney/ ModSimPy/blob/master/examples/kitten.ipynb*.

Simulating a Yo-Yo

Suppose you are holding a yo-yo with a length of string wound around its axle, and you drop it while holding the end of the string stationary. As gravity accelerates the yo-yo downward, tension in the string exerts a force upward. Since this force acts on a point offset from the center of mass, it exerts a torque that causes the yo-yo to spin.

Figure 26-3 shows the forces on the yo-yo and the resulting torque.

The outer shaded area shows the body of the yo-yo. The inner shaded area shows the rolled-up string, the radius of which changes as the yo-yo unrolls.

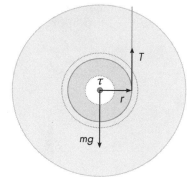

Figure 26-3: A diagram of a yo-yo showing the forces due to gravity and tension in the string, the lever arm of tension, and the resulting torque

In this system, we can't figure out the linear and angular acceleration independently; we have to solve a system of equations:

$$\sum F = ma$$

$$\sum \tau = I\alpha$$

where the summations indicate that we are adding up forces and torques.

As in the previous examples, linear and angular velocity are related because of the way the string unrolls:

$$\frac{dy}{dt} = -r\frac{d\theta}{dt}$$

In this example, the linear and angular accelerations have opposite signs. As the yo-yo rotates counterclockwise, θ increases and y, which is the length of the rolled-up part of the string, decreases.

Taking the derivative of both sides yields a similar relationship between linear and angular acceleration:

$$\frac{d^2y}{dt^2} = -r\frac{d^2\theta}{dt^2}$$

which we can write more concisely:

$$a = -r\alpha$$

This relationship is not a general law of nature; it is specific to scenarios like this, where one object rolls along another without stretching or slipping.

Because of the way we've set up the problem, y actually has two meanings: it represents the length of the rolled string and the height of the yo-yo, which decreases as the yo-yo falls. Similarly, a represents acceleration in the length of the rolled-up string and the height of the yo-yo.

We can compute the acceleration of the yo-yo by adding up the linear forces:

$$\sum F = T - mg = ma$$

where T is positive because the tension force points up, and mg is negative because gravity points down.

Because gravity acts on the center of mass, it creates no torque, so the only torque is due to tension:

$$\sum \tau = Tr = I\alpha$$

Positive (upward) tension yields positive (counterclockwise) angular acceleration.

Now we have three equations with three unknowns, T, a, and α, with I, m, g, and r as known parameters. We could solve these equations by hand, but we can also get SymPy to do it for us:

```
from sympy import symbols, Eq, solve

T, a, alpha, I, m, g, r = symbols('T a alpha I m g r')
eq1 = Eq(a, -r * alpha)
eq2 = Eq(T - m*g, m * a)
eq3 = Eq(T * r, I * alpha)
soln = solve([eq1, eq2, eq3], [T, a, alpha])
soln
```

```
{T: I*g*m/(I + m*r**2), a: -g*m*r**2/(I + m*r**2), alpha: g*m*r/(I + m*r**2)}
```

The results are:

$$T = mgI/I^*$$
$$a = -mgr^2/I^*$$
$$\alpha = mgr/I^*$$

where I^* is the augmented moment of inertia, $I + mr^2$. We can use these equations for a and α to write a slope function and simulate this system.

In the repository for this book, you will find a notebook, *yoyo.ipynb*, which contains starter code you can use to implement and test this model. You can download it from *https://github.com/AllenDowney/ModSimPy/raw/master/examples/yoyo.ipynb* or run it on Colab at *https://colab.research.google.com/github/AllenDowney/ModSimPy/blob/master/examples/yoyo.ipynb*.

Congratulations

With that, you have reached the end of the book, so congratulations! I hope you enjoyed it and learned a lot. I think the tools in this book are useful, and the ways of thinking are important, not just in engineering and science, but in practically every field of inquiry.

Models are the tools we use to understand the world: if you build good models, you are more likely to get things right. Good luck!

APPENDIX

UNDER THE HOOD

In this appendix we'll "open the hood," looking more closely at how some of the tools we have used work: specifically, run_solve_ivp, root_scalar, and maximize_scalar. Most of the time you can use these methods without knowing much about how they work. But there are a few reasons you might *want* to know.

One reason is pure curiosity. If you use these methods, and especially if you come to rely on them, you might find it unsatisfying to treat them as black boxes. In that case, you might enjoy opening the hood.

Another is that these methods are not infallible; sometimes things go wrong. If you know how they work, at least in a general sense, you might find it easier to debug them.

And if nothing else, I have found that I can remember how to use these tools more easily because I know something about how they work.

How run_solve_ivp Works

run_solve_ivp is a function in the ModSim library that checks for common errors in the parameters and then calls solve_ivp, which is the function in the SciPy library that does the actual work.

By default, solve_ivp uses the *Dormand-Prince method*, which is a kind of *Runge-Kutta method*. The key idea behind all Runge-Kutta methods is to evaluate the slope function several times at each time step and use a weighted average of the computed slopes to estimate the value at the next time step. Different methods evaluate the slope function in different places and compute the average with different weights.

So let's see if we can figure out how solve_ivp works. As an example, we'll solve the following differential equation:

$$\frac{dy}{dt}(t) = y \sin t$$

Here's the slope function we'll use:

```
import numpy as np

def slope_func(t, state, system):
    y, = state
    dydt = y * np.sin(t)
    return dydt
```

Let's create a State object with the initial state and a System object with the end time:

```
init = State(y=1)
system = System(init=init, t_end=3)
```

Now we can call run_solve_ivp:

```
results, details = run_solve_ivp(system, slope_func)
details
```

```
message: 'The solver successfully reached the end of the integration interval.'
   nfev: 50
   njev: 0
    nlu: 0
    sol: <scipy.integrate._ivp.common.OdeSolution object at 0x7f4965b8ea10>
 status: 0
success: True
t_events: None
y_events: None
```

One of the variables in details is nfev, which stands for "number of function evaluations," that is, the number of times solve_ivp called the slope function. This example took 50 evaluations. Keep that in mind.

Here are the first few time steps in results:

```
results.head()
```

	y
0.00	1.000000
0.03	1.000450
0.06	1.001801
0.09	1.004055
0.12	1.007217

and here is the number of time steps:

```
len(results)
```

```
101
```

results contains 101 points that are equally spaced in time. Now you might wonder, if solve_ivp ran the slope function 50 times, how did we get 101 time steps?

To answer that question, we need to know more about how the solver works. There are actually three stages:

1. For each time step, solve_ivp evaluates the slope function seven times, with different values of t and y.

2. Using the results, it computes the best estimate for the value y at the next time step.

3. After computing all of the time steps, it uses interpolation to compute equally spaced points that connect the estimates from the previous step.

To show the first two steps, let's modify the slope function so that every time it runs, it adds the values of t, y, and dydt to a list called evals:

```
def slope_func(t, state, system):
    y = state
    dydt = y * np.sin(t)
    evals.append((t, y, dydt))
    return dydt
```

Before we call run_solve_ivp, we'll initialize evals with an empty list. And we'll use the argument dense_output=False, which skips the interpolation step and returns time steps that are not equally spaced (that is, not "dense"):

```
evals = []
results2, details = run_solve_ivp(system, slope_func, dense_output=False)
```

Here are the results:

```
results2
```
----

	y
0.000000	1.000000
0.000100	1.000000
0.001100	1.000001
0.011100	1.000062
0.111100	1.006184
1.111100	1.744448
2.343272	5.464568
3.000000	7.318271

Because we skipped the interpolation step, we can see that solve_ivp computed only seven time steps, not including the initial condition. Also, we see that the time steps are different sizes. The first is only 100 microseconds, the second is about 10 times bigger, and the third is 10 times bigger than that.

The time steps are not equal because the Dormand-Prince method is *adaptive*. At each time step, it computes two estimates of the next value. By comparing them, it can estimate the magnitude of the error, which it uses to adjust the time step. If the error is too big, it uses a smaller time step; if the error is small enough, it uses a bigger time step. By adjusting the time step in this way, it minimizes the number of times it calls the slope function to achieve a given level of accuracy. In this example, it takes five steps to simulate the first second but then only two more steps to compute the remaining two seconds.

Because we saved the values of y and t, we can plot the locations where the slope function was evaluated. I'll need to use a couple of features we have not seen before, if you don't mind.

First we'll unpack the values from evals using np.transpose. Then we can use trigonometry to convert the slope, dydt, to components called u and v:

```
t, y, slope = np.transpose(evals)
theta = np.arctan(slope)
u = np.cos(theta)
v = np.sin(theta)
```

Using these values, we can generate a *quiver plot* that shows an arrow for each time the slope function ran. The location of each arrow represents the values of t and y; the orientation of the arrow shows the slope that was computed:

```
import matplotlib.pyplot as plt

plt.quiver(t, y, u, v, pivot='middle',
          color='C1', alpha=0.4, label='evaluation points')
results2['y'].plot(style='o', color='C0', label='solution points')
```

```
results['y'].plot(lw=1, label='interpolation')

decorate(xlabel='Time (t)',
         ylabel='Quantity (y)')
```

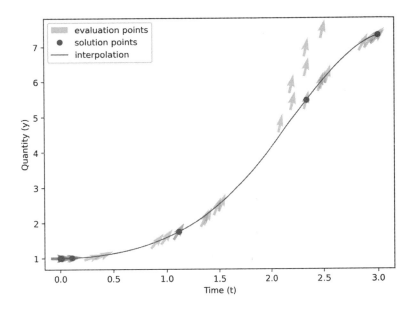

In this figure, there are 50 arrows, one for each time the slope function was evaluated, and 8 dots, one for each time step (although several of them overlap). The line shows the 101 points in the interpolation that connects the estimates.

Notice that many of the arrows do not fall on the line; solve_ivp evaluated the slope function at these locations in order to compute the solution, but as it turned out, they are not part of the solution.

This is good to know when you are writing a slope function—you should not assume that the time and state you get as input variables are correct; that is, they might not turn out to be part of the solution.

How root_scalar Works

root_scalar in the ModSim library is a wrapper for a function in the SciPy library with the same name. Like run_solve_ivp, it checks for common errors and changes some of the parameters in a way that makes the SciPy function easier to use (I hope).

According to the documentation, root_scalar uses Brent's method, which is a combination of bisection, secant, and inverse quadratic interpolation methods (see *https://docs.scipy.org/doc/scipy/reference/generated/scipy.optimize .root_scalar.html*).

To understand what that means, suppose we're trying to find a root of a function of one variable, $f(x)$, and assume we have evaluated the function at two places, x_1 and x_2, and found that the results have opposite signs. Specifically, assume $f(x_1) > 0$ and $f(x_2) < 0$, as shown in Figure A-1.

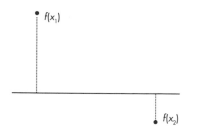
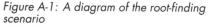

Figure A-1: A diagram of the root-finding scenario

If f is a continuous function, there must be at least one root in this interval. In this case we would say that x_1 and x_2 *bracket* a root.

If this were all you knew about f, where would you go looking for a root? If you said, "halfway between x_1 and x_2," congratulations! You just invented a numerical method called *bisection*!

If you said, "I would connect the dots with a straight line and compute the zero of the line," congratulations! You just invented the *secant method*!

And if you said, "I would evaluate f at a third point, find the parabola that passes through all three points, and compute the zeros of the parabola," congratulations! You just invented *inverse quadratic interpolation*!

That's most of how `root_scalar` works. The details of how these methods are combined are interesting but beyond the scope of this book. You can read more at *https://en.wikipedia.org/wiki/Brents_method*.

How maximize_scalar Works

`maximize_scalar` in the ModSim library is a wrapper for a function in the SciPy library called `minimize_scalar`. You can read about it at *https://docs.scipy.org/ doc/scipy/reference/generated/scipy.optimize.minimize_scalar.html*.

By default, it uses Brent's method, which is related to the method I described in the previous section for root-finding. Brent's method for finding a maximum or minimum is based on a simpler algorithm: the *golden-section search*, which I will explain.

Suppose we're trying to find the minimum of a function of a single variable, $f(x)$. As a starting place, assume that we have evaluated the function at three places, x_1, x_2, and x_3, and found that x_2 yields the lowest value. Figure A-2 shows this initial state.

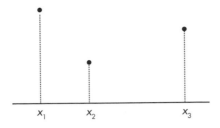

Figure A-2: A diagram of the initial state of
a minimization algorithm

We will assume that $f(x)$ is continuous and *unimodal* in this range, which means that there is exactly one minimum between x_1 and x_3.

The next step is to choose a fourth point, x_4, and evaluate $f(x_4)$. There are two possible outcomes, depending on whether $f(x_4)$ is greater than $f(x_2)$ or not. Figure A-3 shows the two possible states.

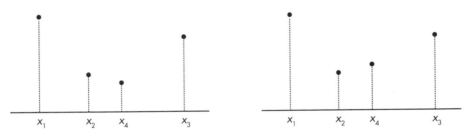

Figure A-3: A diagram of two possible states of a minimization algorithm

If $f(x_4)$ is less than $f(x_2)$ (shown on the left), the minimum must be between x_2 and x_3, so we would discard x_1 and proceed with the new bracket (x_2, x_4, x_3).

If $f(x_4)$ is greater than $f(x_2)$ (shown on the right), the local minimum must be between x_1 and x_4, so we would discard x_3 and proceed with the new bracket (x_1, x_2, x_4).

Either way, the range gets smaller and our estimate of the optimal value of x gets better.

This method works for almost any value of x_4, but some choices are better than others. You might be tempted to bisect the interval between x_2 and x_3, but that turns out not to be optimal. You can read about a better option at *https://greenteapress.com/matlab/golden*.

INDEX

A

absolute error, 47
abstraction, 4, 10
acceleration, 172, 181, 192
   due to gravity, 173, 228
   of gravity, 5
adaptive time step, 238
air resistance, 6, 176, 177, 196
American Museum of Natural History, 43
Anaconda, xxv–xxvi
analysis, mathematical, 4, 10, 82, 123, 141
angle, 187
angular acceleration, 215, 219, 232
angular velocity, 207
animation, 196, 225
append function, 221
argument, 21
   function as, 58
array, 37, 132, 142
Ask an Astronomer, 176
assignment, multiple, 100
assignment operator, 31
assumption, modeling, 28
attribute, 25

B

bag of blood model, 157
barometric pressure, 179
baseball, 12, 185, 189
basic reproduction number, 122
bike share model, 27
bike share system, 15
bisection method, 240
blood sugar, 146
body (of function), 17
Boolean value, 19
Boston, Massachusetts, 200
Boston Red Sox, 200
Box, George, 6, 27
bracket (a root), 134, 224, 240

bracket operator, 48, 187
Brent's method, 240
brick wall, 166
bungee jump, 227

C

calculus, xx
carrying capacity, 65, 71
Census Bureau, 45
circuit diagram, 164
circumference, 206
clobber, 66
code block, 17
coefficient of friction, 217
coffee cooling problem, 127
comment, 29
comparison operators, 31
compartment models, 97
component of vector, 186
conduction, 129
conservation of energy, 138
constant growth model, 79
constant of integration, 81
contact number, 122
continuous model, 81
continuous time, 142
contour plot, 116
convection, 129
crossings function, 175
cross product, 215

D

DataFrame object, 44
debugging, 40
decorate function, 24
degree, 188
density, 178
Denver, Colorado, 197
derivative, 212
deterministic model, 32
diabetes mellitus, 146

diagram, stock and flow, 97
diameter, 179
difference equation, 80, 131, 158
differential equation, 81, 97, 122, 131,
158, 164, 165, 171, 208
DimensionalityError, 11
dimensionless, 120, 178
direction (of vector), 186, 215
discrete, 124, 142
discrete model, 81
DNA, 147
docstring, 29
documentation, 29
Dormand-Prince method, 236
dot operator, 16, 45, 186
drag coefficient, 178, 185
drag equation, 178, 181
drag force, 177, 181, 191, 196
dynamical systems, xix

E

Earth, 176, 229
else clause, 20
Empire State Building, 5, 172, 229
equals operator, 31
equation
    difference, 80, 131, 158
    differential, 81, 97, 122, 131, 158,
    164, 165, 171, 208
equilibrium, 65
Erlich, Paul, 43
error function, 135, 223
errors
    absolute, 47
    DimensionalityError, 11
    NameError, 67
    relative, 48
    syntax, 11, 31
    ValueError, 134
Euler's method, 158
event function, 175, 192, 208, 220
exponential function, 81
exponential growth, 88
exponentiation, 6

F

falling penny myth, 172
Fenway Park, 200

filter, 165
first-order differential equation, 171
flip function, 19, 26
flows, 97
force, 172, 192, 215
    drag, 177, 181, 191, 196
for loop, 22
format specifier, 112
formatted string literal, 112
framework, modeling, 3, 10
free parameters, 63, 148
frequently sampled intravenous
    glucose tolerance test (FSIGT),
    146
Freshman Plague, 95, 125
friction, 217, 224, 230
f-string, 112
function
    append, 221
    as argument, 58
    body of, 17
    call, 17
    common errors, 65
    crossings, 175
    decorate, 24
    definition, 17
    error, 135, 223
    event, 175, 192, 208, 220
    exponential, 81
    flip, 19, 26
    generalization of, 21
    head, 44
    interpolate, 149
    leastsq, 163
    linspace, 37
    make_series, 123
    maximize_scalar, 201, 240
    as parameter, 58, 134
    plot, 24, 64
    range, 22, 37
    read_html, 44
    root of, 65, 134
    as return value, 149
    root_scalar, 134, 218, 224, 239
    run_solve_ivp, 159, 236
    slope, 159, 173, 180, 191, 208
    sqrt, 7
    State, 16
    tail, 45

unimodal, 241
Vector, 186
zero of, 65

G

gene, 147
generalization of a function, 21
general solution, 85
glucose, 146
golden-section search, 240
gravity, 5, 173, 228, 231, 233
Green Monster, 200
growth rate, 65
gyroscopic precession, 205

H

hardcoding, 49
head function, 44
heat, 128
heat flux, 166
herd immunity, 109
HIV, 167
homeostasis, 146
Hooke's law, 228
humidity, 179
hyperglycemia, 146
hypothetical entity, 147

I

if statement, 19
iloc, 132
immune response, 167
immunization, 106
implementation, 98, 153
incremental development, 40, 91
index (of Series), 45
initial value problem, 159
insulin, 146
    minimal model, 164
integration, 81, 123, 212
International System of Units, 8
interpolate function, 149
interpolation, 149, 238
inverse quadratic interpolation, 240
iterative modeling, 5, 28

J

joule, 128
Jupyter, xxiv–xxvi

K

Kermack-McKendrick model, 96
Kirchhoff's current law, 165
kitten, 230

L

label, 23
launch angle, 201
law of nature, 130
law of universal gravitation, 176
leastsq function, 163
lever arm, 215
libraries
    Matplotlib, 26, 42, 64, 116, 225
    ModSim, xxi, 16, 59, 116, 123, 126,
        134, 159, 175, 186, 196, 201
    NumPy, 7, 37, 188
    pandas, 25, 42, 44, 126, 148
    Pint, 8
    SciPy, 151, 159, 163, 236, 239, 240
    SymPy, 83, 233
    types, 59
linear growth, 88
linear interpolation, 150
linear relationship, 62
linspace function, 37
loc, 103, 132
logarithm, 81, 141
logistic growth, 87, 88
loop variable, 22
low-pass filter, 164

M

magnitude, 9, 186–187, 215
Magnus force, 185
make_series function, 123
Mars Climate Orbiter, 8
mass, 172, 216
Mathematica, 83
mathematical constant, pi, 11
mathematical notation, 83, 155

Matplotlib library, 26, 42, 64, 116, 225
maximize_scalar function, 201, 240
maximize_scalar object, 201
metric, 32, 107
minimal model, 146, 164
mixture of liquids, 138
modeling, iterative, 5, 28
modeling decision, 130, 185
modeling framework, 3, 10
models, 4
    bag of blood, 157
    bike share, 27
    compartment, 97
    constant growth, 79
    continuous, 81
    deterministic, 32
    discrete, 81
    Kermack-McKendrick, 96
    minimal, 146, 164
    nonspatial, 157
    proportional, 80
    quadratic, 65, 80
    SIR, 96
    stochastic, 32
ModSim library, xxi, 16, 59, 116, 123,
        126, 134, 159, 175, 186, 196,
        201
moment of inertia, 216
Moore, Lang, 95
Mount Everest, 129
multiple assignment, 100
multiplication, 6
MythBusters, 6, 178

N

NameError, 67
NaN value, 45
natural law, 130
net growth (population), 64
Newton's law of cooling, 129
Newton's law of universal gravitation,
        5
Newton's second law of motion, 172,
        216
Newton's third law of motion, 177
nondimensionalization, 120
None value, 67

nonspatial model, 157
notebook, Jupyter, xxiv–xxvi
NumPy library, 7, 11, 37, 188

O

objects
    DataFrame, 44
    maximize_scalar, 201
    OdeResult, 159
    Params, 178
    Series, 25, 42
    SimpleNamespace, 59
    State, 16, 28
    SweepFrame, 114
    SweepSeries, 38
    Symbol, 83
    System, 53
    TimeFrame, 101
    TimeSeries, 22
    UnitRegistry, 8
    Vector, 186
Occam's razor, 146
OdeResult object, 159
Ohm's law, 165
Olin College, 15, 95
operators
    assignment, 31
    bracket, 48, 187
    comparison, 31
    dot, 16, 45, 186
    equals, 31
    update, 16
optimization, 204, 230, 240
orbit, 229
Orwell, George, 27

P

pandas library, 25, 42, 44, 126, 148
parabola, 175, 213
parameter, 21, 28
    free, 63, 148
    function as, 58, 134
    model vs. function, 37
    sweeping, 38, 108, 113, 140
    system, 53
parameterize, 65, 80

Params object, 178
particular solution, 85
penny myth, 3, 5
pharmacokinetics, 146
Phillips, Andrew, 167
physical system, 4
Physics of Baseball, The, 185, 189, 197
pi, 11
Pint library, 8
Pint quantity, 9
planetary orbit, 4, 229
plot function, 24, 64
pole, 10-foot, 11
population, 43
Population Bomb, The, 43
position, 171
precession, 205
precision, 7
print statement, 18
programming language, 83
projection, 69
    vs. prediction, 71
proportional model, 80

Q

quadratic model, 65, 80
quadratic relationship, 62
quality of fit, 57
quantity, 9
    vector, 186, 215
quarantine, 110
quarter exercise, 183
queueing theory, 90
quiver plot, 238

R

radian, 188, 207
radiation, 129
Ramirez, Manny, 200
random number generator, 19, 26
range (of trajectory), 201, 230
range function, 22, 37
read_html function, 44
reference area, 178
relative error, 48, 161
return statement, 30, 36, 67
return value, 36
root (of function), 65, 134

root_scalar function, 134, 218, 224, 239
Rosling, Hans, 74
rotation, 206
Rothstein, Dave, 176
run_solve_ivp function, 159, 236
Runge-Kutta method, 236
running a race, 13

S

salmon population, 91
scaffolding, 40
Scientific American, 127
scientific notation, 45
SciPy library, 151, 159, 163, 236, 239, 240
secant method, 240
second-order differential equation, 171
Series object, 25, 42, 45
signal, 165
SI units, 8, 128
SimpleNamespace object, 59
simulation, 4, 10, 82, 123
SIR model, 96
site index (tree growth), 92
slope function, 159, 173, 180, 191, 208
Smith, David, 95
specific heat capacity, 128, 138
Spider-Man, 229
spring constant, 228
sqrt function, 7
square root, 7
state (of system), 16
State function, 16
statements
    if, 19
    print, 18
    return, 30, 36, 67
State object, 16, 28
state variable, 16, 173, 208, 218
stochastic model, 32
stock and flow diagram, 97
stocks, 97
string, 18
Sun, 176, 229
SweepFrame object, 114
sweeping a parameter, 38, 108, 113, 140

SweepSeries object, 38
Symbol object, 83
SymPy library, 83, 233
syntax error, 11, 31
system, physical, 4
System object, 53
system of equations, 232
system parameter, 53
system state, 16

T

tail function, 45
temperature, 128, 166
tension, 231
tensor, 216
terminal velocity, 6, 178
thermal mass, 128, 138, 166
thermal resistance, 166
thermal systems, 127, 166
TimeFrame object, 101
TimeSeries object, 22
timestamp, 22
time step, 20, 90, 131, 158, 162, 238
toilet paper roll, physics of, 206, 230
torque, 215, 224, 231
traceback, 12
trajectory, 230
trajectory plot, 195
tree growth, 92
turntable, 216
types library, 59

U

UN DESA, 46
unimodal function, 241
United Nations Department of
        Economic and Social Affairs
        (UN DESA), 46
United States Census Bureau, 45

UnitRegistry object, 8
units, 8, 128
unit vector, 188
update operator, 16
US Atlantic Salmon Assessment
        Committee, 91

V

vaccine, 105
validation, 4, 10, 143, 158
    external, 5
    internal, 5
value, 6
    Boolean, 19
    NaN, 45
    None, 67
    return, 36
ValueError, 134
variable, 6
    loop, 22
    state, 16, 173, 208, 218
Vector object, 186
vector quantity, 186, 215
velocity, 171, 178

W

Walker, Jearl, 127
Wellesley College, 15
Wikipedia, 44
WolframAlpha, 83
world population, 43, 89

Y

yo-yo example, 231

Z

zero (of function), 65

The fonts used in *Modeling and Simulation in Python* are New Baskerville, Futura, The Sans Mono Condensed, and Dogma. The book was typeset with LaTeX 2_ε package nostarch by Boris Veytsman *(2008/06/06 v1.3 Typesetting books for No Starch Press)*.

RESOURCES

Visit *https://nostarch.com/modeling-and-simulation-python* for errata and more information.

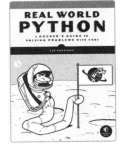

Never before has the world relied so heavily on the Internet
to stay connected and informed. That makes the Electronic
Frontier Foundation's mission—to ensure that technology
supports freedom, justice, and innovation for all people—
more urgent than ever.

For over 30 years, EFF has fought for tech users through
activism, in the courts, and by developing software to overcome
obstacles to your privacy, security, and free expression. This
dedication empowers all of us through darkness. With your help
we can navigate toward a brighter digital future.